THE SEVEN *M*'S OF MISSIONARY SERVICE

THE SEVEN *M*'S OF MISSIONARY SERVICE

CARLOS E. ASAY

BOOKCRAFT
SALT LAKE CITY, UTAH

Library of Congress Catalog Card Number: 96-86337
ISBN 1-57008-287-1

First Printing, 1996

Printed in the United States of America

CONTENTS

ACKNOWLEDGMENTS

Several years ago I was privileged to serve as the executive director of the Missionary Department of The Church of Jesus Christ of Latter-day Saints. This assignment provided me many opportunities to tour missions, interview missionaries and mission presidents, attend seminars for mission presidents and wives, and do other things that exposed me to all facets of this fascinating and vibrant arm of Church service. The assignment also enabled me to associate rather closely with great missionary leaders such as President Spencer W. Kimball, President Gordon B. Hinckley, President Thomas S. Monson, and a long line of mission presidents who have given inspired direction to the proselyting efforts of the Church.

More than once, I have heard leaders, particularly President Thomas S. Monson, speak of what they term the "M's of missionary service." Sometimes the list of M's has been short, numbering only three or four dimensions of the work. Sometimes the list has been longer. But always I have been intrigued by the discussion of key or pivotal words that helped listeners piece together and remember the essential elements of the charge to teach all nations, kindreds, tongues, and people.

I have therefore compiled my own list of "M's" pertaining to missionary service. The list began with five, exploded to ten, and finally settled at seven. There is nothing sacred about my list of seven; however, I do feel strongly that I have identified the most crucial parts of a work that began "from the beginning" (Moses 5:58) and will continue until the Great Jehovah declares it accomplished.

If there is anything unique about this book, it is the attempt to describe missionary service for both member-missionaries and full-time missionaries. All have the responsibility to teach, testify, and exemplify gospel truths. All are expected to catch the spirit and vision of missionary service and to seek for the merits of this most sanctifying work, for it is the means of saving ourselves and those who hear us (see 1 Timothy 4:16).

In this book members are referred to as "multiplying factors" in missionary service. This expression suggests that the proselyting efforts of the Church will be multiplied many times over when all of the Saints become active participants in sharing the gospel and working in a balanced, harmonious way with full-time missionaries. Therefore, the M's of missionary service presented in this book apply to members and full-time missionaries alike.

It is proper to note that portions of the material included within these covers were published in my previous book titled *In the Lord's Service* (Salt Lake City: Deseret Book Co., 1990)—a book that is now out of print. It is the author's considered opinion that the republished materials take on deeper meaning in the context of discussions related to missionary service.

I am indebted to many who have assisted me with this publication. As previously mentioned, President Monson and others planted the ideas in my mind. My wife, Colleen; my secretary, Margie McKnight; and editors Christopher K. Bigelow and Rebecca M. Taylor nourished the project by lending encouragement and professional assistance. But in the end, I like to think that it is the Lord who has given the increase from the conception of the idea to the completion of the book.

This is not an official Church publication. I assume full and personal responsibility for the contents and organization of this book.

"GO YE INTO ALL THE WORLD, AND PREACH THE GOSPEL TO EVERY CREATURE"

Soon after his crucifixion, the risen Christ met his disciples on a mountain in Galilee and said: "Go ye therefore, and teach all nations, baptizing them in the name of the Father, and of the Son, and of the Holy Ghost: teaching them to observe all things whatsoever I have commanded you: and, lo, I am with you alway, even unto the end of the world" (Matthew 28:19–20).

This divine commission was all-inclusive and long-standing in purpose. It obligated Jesus' disciples to seek out and teach "all nations, kindreds, tongues, and people" (D&C 112:1), not just a select few. It also implied an ongoing task of great importance that must be pursued relentlessly until completed, "for the eternal purposes of the Lord shall roll on, until all his promises shall be fulfilled" (Mormon 8:22).

Peter, James, John, and others were loyal to the Master and true to the charge given them. They forsook all and fearlessly shared the glad tidings of the gospel with both Jew and Gentile. In due time, Christ's little band of missionaries was joined by Paul, Philip, Silas, and a few more. Just how far their travels took them we are not certain. Nor are we sure of the number of converts won by these men who were accused of turning the "world upside down" (Acts 17:6). We do know, however, that persecution nipped at their heels most of the way as they carried their message into the old Roman world and visited places such as Antioch, Athens, and Rome. Nonetheless, "they went forth, and preached every where, the Lord working with them, and confirming the word with signs following" (Mark 16:20).

Some listeners "were pricked in their heart" by the words of Peter and the rest of the Apostles and asked, "Men and brethren, what shall we do?" (Acts 2:37.) One listener said of Philip, "This man is the great power of God" (Acts 8:10). After Paul gave a speech, it was said of him, "The gods are come down to us in the likeness of men" (Acts 14:11). Paul's stirring words even caused King Agrippa to confess, "Almost thou persuadest me to be a Christian" (Acts 26:28).

Apostasy

As "the word of God grew and multiplied" (Acts 12:24) in the meridian of time through the efforts of Christ's disciples, so did opposition. Paul counseled the Saints in Corinth, "Watch ye, stand fast in the faith" (1 Corinthians 16:13). He warned the Galatians to avoid preachers of false gospels. He wrote the Ephesians about the need to cling to the Church and follow its officers so they wouldn't be "tossed to and fro, and carried about with every wind of doctrine" (Ephesians 4:14). He encouraged the Colossians to be "rooted and built up" in Christ and thus avoid the spoiling philosophies and traditions of men (Colossians 2:7–8). Still, Paul knew that an apostasy would occur before Christ's second coming. He said: "For that day shall not come, except there come a falling away first, and that man of sin be revealed, the son of perdition" (2 Thessalonians 2:3).

That sad day surely did come when grievous wolves entered in among the Christian flock. By the close of the first century after the death of Christ, all of the Apostles had been killed and a long night of spiritual darkness blanketed the earth. Before long, the people had "transgressed the laws, changed the ordinance, broken the everlasting covenant," just as Isaiah predicted they would (Isaiah 24:5). The early Christian church became splintered, antichrists and false prophets appeared on the scene, and some men claimed to be Apostles but were found to be liars (see 1 John 2:18; Revelation 2:2). Thus, the days came when there was "a famine in the land, not a famine of bread, nor a thirst for water, but of hearing the words of the Lord" (Amos 8:11).

Many volumes have been written describing the Great Apostasy wherein pagan practices and other worldly influences diluted the early Christian doctrine. Eventually, the priesthood was lost, the gifts of the Spirit were no longer manifested, and the pure love of God waxed cold. Ultimately, the gospel taught by Christ and his Apostles was perverted almost beyond recognition and the church established by the Master was spiritually razed by men with ulterior motives.

Reformation

The long night of spiritual darkness, sometimes referred to as the Dark Ages, when people suffered in ignorance and sin, continued for several centuries. Gradually, however, men were raised up who sought added enlightenment and who had hopes for the future. Luther, Calvin, Knox, and others rebelled against the apostate religions of their day and worked toward a restoration of pure doctrine and practices among so-called Christians.

Each of the reformers of the 16th century, whether he realized it or not, was prompted by the Spirit to initiate actions that over time would cumulatively break the bonds that held truth seekers captive. Such actions were a prelude to the restoration of the gospel as foretold by holy prophets. Isaiah forecasted a day when God would "recover the remnant of his people" (Isaiah 11:11) and "do a marvellous work among this people, even a marvellous work and a wonder" (Isaiah 29:14). Malachi spoke of a time when God would send "Elijah the prophet before the coming of the great and dreadful day of the Lord" (Malachi 4:5). Peter declared that there would be a time of "restitution of all things, which God hath spoken by the mouth of all his holy prophets since the world began" (Acts 3:21). John saw in vision "another angel fly in the midst of heaven, having the everlasting gospel to preach unto them that dwell on the earth, and to every nation, and kindred, and tongue, and people" (Revelation 14:6). All of these prophecies and more were to be fulfilled by a loving God who was ready to respond to the prayers and desires of his righteous children.

Restoration

The angel seen by John did fly; the restitution of all things predicted by Peter did occur; and as Malachi forecasted, Elijah and other
heavenly messengers were sent by God to the earth. The restoration
of the gospel of Jesus Christ began with the first vision of the Prophet
Joseph Smith—a vision involving a boy, God the Father, and God the
Son. The Restoration progressed with the appearance of the angel
Moroni and the coming forth of the Book of Mormon—Another
Testament of Jesus Christ. The Restoration reached a high crescendo
when the priesthood, or power to act in the name of God, was restored by John the Baptist (Aaronic Priesthood) and by Peter, James,
and John (Melchizedek Priesthood). Joseph Smith's restorative work
climaxed with the establishment of The Church of Jesus Christ of
Latter-day Saints in 1830.

Our Divine Commission

Once the gospel in its fulness and original purity had been restored
and the Church re-established, it is understandable that the Lord
would reissue through his prophet the divine commission to spread the
truth. In 1831 he declared to the people living in the modern world:
"And this gospel shall be preached unto every nation, and kindred,
and tongue, and people. And the servants of God shall go forth, saying
with a loud voice: Fear God and give glory to him, for the hour of his
judgment is come; and worship him that made heaven, and earth, and
the sea, and the fountains of waters" (D&C 133:37–39).

Much like the charge given his disciples in the meridian of time,
the Savior's charge given in the fulness of times was issued in clear
and unmistakable terms. The servants of God will preach the truth
throughout the world! All will be given an opportunity to worship
the true and living God! This knowledge prompted a modern prophet
to proclaim: "Our missionaries are going forth to different nations, . . .
the Standard of Truth has been erected; no unhallowed hand can stop
the work from progressing; persecutions may rage, mobs may com-
bine, armies may assemble, calumny may defame, but the truth of
God will go forth boldly, nobly, and independent, till it has pene-
trated every continent, visited every clime, swept every country, and
sounded in every ear, till the purposes of God shall be accomplished,

and the Great Jehovah shall say the work is done" (in *History of the Church* 4:540).

Invitation

In reality, the divine commission given Christ's disciples in the meridian of time and reiterated in modern times is a divine invitation—an invitation to come unto Christ. It is written: "Behold, he sendeth an invitation unto all men, for the arms of mercy are extended towards them, and he said: Repent, and I will receive you. Yea, he saith: *Come unto me* and ye shall partake of the fruit of the tree of life; yea, ye shall eat and drink of the bread and the waters of life freely; yea, *come unto me* and bring forth works of righteousness." (Alma 5:33–35; emphasis added.)

Speaking to the members of the Church, Elder Stephen L Richards described the divine invitation in laymen's terms. The invitation he proposed reads as follows:

To: All Men, Women, and Children . . .

You are cordially and earnestly invited to participate in building the kingdom of God in the earth.

Place—Everywhere.
Time—Now.
Signed—The Church of Jesus Christ of Latter-day Saints.

(In Conference Report, October 1952, pp. 97–98.)

Seven M's of Missionary Service

The divine commission to share the gospel is not the exclusive right of only a privileged few, nor is it an onerous responsibility to be shouldered alone by apostles and prophets. It is the right and responsibility of all who have embraced the restored gospel. I do, therefore, address this book to all Latter-day Saints, reminding them that they are expected—even commanded—to invite others to come unto Christ (see Alma 5:62).

I propose that the seven most significant M's of missionary service are:

- Mankind: "The Whole Human Family of Adam" (Mormon 3:20)
- Message: "Come Unto Christ, . . . and Partake of His Salvation" (Omni 1:26)
- Members: Every Member a Missionary
- Missionaries: Missionaries to Match the Message
- Methods: Use of Every Honorable Means
- Motivation: Motivation that Comes of True Conversion
- Merits: A Treasure Chest of Blessings

Other aspects of missionary service might be proposed and discussed. The list could include media, machines, and other unmentioned approaches. However, the seven topics selected for treatment in this book seem to be "things as they really are, and . . . things as they really will be" (Jacob 4:13) as pertaining to missionary service.

THE SPIRIT AND VISION OF MISSIONARY SERVICE

The Spirit of Missionary Service

Several years ago I received an assignment to attend a conference in the eastern part of the United States. I made the proper arrangements with the expectations that all would go according to my well-laid plans. But when the day of departure arrived, everything seemed to come unraveled, and I boarded the airplane with a sagging spirit and in a less than congenial mood.

I took my assigned seat on the plane, opened my briefcase, and began to work on some materials that required careful review. It pleased me to observe that the seat next to mine was not occupied. This raised my hopes of traveling undisturbed by idle conversation with some stranger.

Just moments before the boarding gate was closed, a very hairy and unkempt young man rushed through the doorway, swept by the flight attendants, and took the only remaining seat—the one next to mine. I must admit that this turn of events annoyed me. Not only had I lost the privacy I wanted, but I was now crowded next to a person who appeared worldly, smelled of oil and grease, and seemed eager for conversation.

I ignored the intruder and continued with my reading. I even turned obliquely in my seat away from the man, hoping that the positioning of my body would send a signal that might keep him at bay.

Once the airplane was off the ground and had reached its flying altitude, my unwelcomed traveling companion turned to me and said, "I fear that I may have offended you, and I want to explain why I look so grubby." He then explained that he was from New York and had been attending an auto mechanics seminar in Utah—a seminar that concluded with a hands-on workshop. He further explained that the workshop concluded only a few minutes before the time of departure from Salt Lake City and that he had not been provided the time to change clothes, wash, and make himself more presentable. He concluded by saying, "I hope that you will forgive me for the way I look and smell."

Oh, how very ashamed I was! Ashamed that I had prejudged a man; ashamed that I had been so selfish in my desires and behavior; and ashamed that I had carried a spirit so contrary to my calling.

I introduced myself and apologized for my aloofness. He accepted my apology graciously. Soon we were engaged in a conversation wherein we both talked about family, church, and other important things. Eventually we opened the scriptures and discussed the restored gospel with an openness usually reserved for old friends. Upon arrival at our destination, we parted company with a warm handshake and the promise that he would receive representatives of the LDS Church, whom I would send.

I shall never forget the swing of mood and the change in spirit that came over me as I pushed aside my own selfish interests, became genuinely interested in a very fine young man, and began to share with him my faith in God. This experience served to remind me that we should not prejudge others despite outward appearances. It also reminded me that when we live outside of ourselves and attempt to share the gospel of Jesus Christ with others, a beautiful spirit comes into our presence. It is the spirit of testimony, the spirit of the scriptures, and the spirit of brotherhood that hover over and around all honest missionary efforts.

"Desirous that [Others] Should Partake"

When Church members and missionaries are touched by that spirit of which I speak, they have a compelling desire to *share*, as expressed by father Lehi: "I did go forth and partake of the fruit thereof;

and I beheld that it was most sweet, above all that I ever before tasted. Yea, and I beheld that the fruit thereof was white, to exceed all the whiteness that I had ever seen.

"And as I partook of the fruit thereof it filled my soul with exceedingly great joy; wherefore, I began to be desirous that my family should partake of it also; for I knew that it was desirable above all other fruit." (1 Nephi 8:11–12.)

"Desirous that Salvation Should Be Declared"

When Church members and missionaries are touched by the missionary spirit, they feel a *desire* for the welfare of others similar to that demonstrated by the repentant sons of Mosiah. Of them it was written:

"Now they were desirous that salvation should be declared to every creature, for they could not bear that any human soul should perish; yea, even the very thoughts that any soul should endure endless torment did cause them to quake and tremble. And thus did the Spirit of the Lord work upon them." (Mosiah 28:3–4.)

"Wish of Mine Heart"

When Church members and missionaries are touched by the missionary spirit, they *wish* for the same thing that Alma did. He cried out: "O that I were an angel, and could have the wish of mine heart, that I might go forth and speak with the trump of God, with a voice to shake the earth, and cry repentance unto every people! Yea, I would declare unto every soul, as with the voice of thunder, repentance and the plan of redemption, that they should repent and come unto our God, that there might not be more sorrow upon all the face of the earth." (Alma 29:1–2.)

"Their Souls Are Precious"

When Church members and missionaries are touched by the missionary spirit, they *pray* as Alma prayed: "O Lord, wilt thou grant unto us that we may have success in bringing them again unto thee in Christ. Behold, O Lord, their souls are precious, and many of them are our brethren; therefore, give unto us, O Lord, power and wisdom that we may bring these, our brethren, again unto thee." (Alma 31:34–35.)

"Ye Were Dear unto Us"

When Church members and missionaries are touched by the missionary spirit, they *express* the kind of love that the Apostle Paul expressed to the people in Thessalonica: "Being affectionately desirous of you, we were willing to have imparted unto you, not the gospel of God only, but also our own souls, because ye were dear unto us" (1 Thessalonians 2:8).

"Cry from the Morning, Even Until . . ."

When Church members and missionaries are touched by the missionary spirit, they *work* as Ether worked: "Ether . . . began to prophesy unto the people, for he could not be restrained because of the Spirit of the Lord which was in him. For he did cry from the morning, even until the going down of the sun, exhorting the people to believe in God unto repentance lest they should be destroyed, saying unto them that by faith all things are fulfilled." (Ether 12:2–3.)

The missionary spirit described in the above-mentioned scriptures was not the sole possession of the ancients or something reserved for people of past generations. Modern exponents of the truth have also enjoyed the companionship of that spirit.

"I Wanted to Thunder and Roar"

Once converted, Brigham Young said: "I wanted to thunder and roar out the Gospel to the nations. It burned in my bones like fire pent up, so I turned my back upon Jackson County to preach the Gospel of life to the people. . . . Nothing would satisfy me but to cry abroad in the world, what the Lord was doing in the latter days." (In *Journal of Discourses* 1:313.)

"I Can Never Rest Till . . ."

Soon after he became an active participant in the Lord's service, Parley P. Pratt preached: "If I had been set to turn the world over, to dig down a mountain, to go to the ends of the earth, or traverse the deserts of Arabia, it would have been easier than to have undertaken to rest, while the Priesthood was upon me. I have received the holy anointing, and I can never rest till the last enemy is conquered, death destroyed, and truth reigns triumphant." (In *Journal of Discourses* 1:15.)

"Irresistible Urge"

During his distinguished ministry, Elder Marion G. Romney stated: "No person whose soul is illuminated by the burning Spirit of God can in this world of sin and dense darkness remain passive. He is driven by an irresistible urge to fit himself to be an active agent of God in furthering righteousness and in freeing the lives and minds of men from the bondage of sin." (In Conference Report, October 1941, p. 89.)

I've written elsewhere that there is an irresistible urge and a lifting spirit associated with missionary service regardless of whether you are a member-missionary or a full-time missionary. I'm convinced that each time we walk our roads to Emmaus, talking and opening up the scriptures to others, our views of gospel truths are expanded and our hearts burn a little brighter. I am convinced that each time we extend the right hand of friendship and fellowship to the lame in body and spirit at our "Beautiful Gates" and lift people up, we stand a little straighter, walk with a spring in our step, and praise God with greater fervor. I'm convinced that each time we visit our Jacob's wells and invite friends to drink of living waters, our thirst is quenched and we draw closer to the Savior of the world. (See Carlos E. Asay, *In the Lord's Service* [Salt Lake City: Deseret Book Co., 1990], p. 43.) Just as the spirit or breath of life animates the human body, so does the Spirit of God give life and vitality to all who engage in missionary service.

Lehi, the sons of Mosiah, Alma, Ether, Brigham Young, Parley P. Pratt, and many others attest to the fact that a marvelous phenomenon occurs in the lives of people when the spirit of missionary service rests upon them. Almost instinctively, it seems, that spirit sparks a

compelling desire, even an incessant wish, to share truths and testimonies. When our minds are expanded by new knowledge, we want
others to know. When our spirits are elevated by uplifting influences, we
want others to feel. When our lives are filled with goodness, we want
others, particularly those whom we love, to enjoy similar experiences.

I once heard the testimony of a new convert, a young man obviously touched by the Spirit. Among other things, he indicated that it
was his great desire to share the restored gospel with his family and
friends. With tears in his eyes and a quiver in his voice, he said: "I
want them to know what I know. I want them to feel what I feel. I
want them to do what I have done."

The Vision of Missionary Service

In the Old Testament we read of a time when the king of Syria
waged war against Israel. On two occasions the Syrian army was positioned for a surprise attack and certain victory. The victories, however, did not come; for Elisha, a man of God, warned the king of Israel
and revealed the place of the Syrian encampment.

When the king of Syria learned that Elisha was the cause of his
frustrations, he sent spies to locate the prophet. He was informed that
Elisha was at a city called Dothan. Under cover of night, he sent a
great host of horses and chariots and surrounded Dothan and its inhabitants, hoping that he might capture Elisha.

Very early in the morning, Elisha and his servant arose and discovered that they were encircled by the enemy. The frightened servant exclaimed: "Alas, my master! how shall we do?" Elisha answered
in a reassuring voice: "Fear not: for they that be with us are more than
they that be with them." Then Elisha prayed and said: "Lord, I pray
thee, *open his eyes*, that he may see." The young man's eyes were
opened, and he saw that "the mountain was full of horses and chariots
of fire round about Elisha." (2 Kings 6:8–18; emphasis added.)

I suspect there are times when Latter-day Saints feel much like
Elisha's servant. They, too, are engaged in a war for the souls of men
and are surrounded by the great host of horses and chariots of the evil
one. At times the forces pitted against them seem almost overwhelm-
ing, causing many to wonder about the outcome of the battle. The
faint of heart stand apart and ask, "How shall we do?"

Church of the Lamb of God

As Elisha prayed for his frightened servant, so the Brethren pray for members whose eyes have not yet been opened to the vista of this great latter-day work in which we are involved. I want to share with you some scriptures and quotations of living prophets that reveal the true destiny of the church of the Lamb—a destiny that will be realized as members and missionaries catch the vision of missionary service and do their part.

You will recall that Father Lehi received a spiritual manifestation of great significance, referred to as the vision of the tree of life. Afterwards he shared his remarkable experience with members of his family. Some of Lehi's sons regarded lightly his teachings. Others, those with receptive hearts, desired to know more concerning the future of the Lord's work.

Such was the case with Nephi. He was touched by the power of the Holy Ghost, and he, too, was desirous that he "might see, and hear, and know" (1 Nephi 10:17). Not only was Nephi permitted to see in vision that which father Lehi had seen, but other truths and glorious views concerning the latter days were revealed, including this glimpse of the future:

> And it came to pass that I beheld the church of the Lamb of God, and its numbers were few, because of the wickedness and abominations of the whore who sat upon many waters; nevertheless, I beheld that the church of the Lamb, who were the saints of God, were also upon all the face of the earth; and their dominions upon the face of the earth were small, because of the wickedness of the great whore whom I saw.
>
> And it came to pass that I beheld that the great mother of abominations did gather together multitudes upon the face of all the earth, among all the nations of the Gentiles, to fight against the Lamb of God.
>
> And it came to pass that I, Nephi, beheld the power of the Lamb of God, that it descended upon the saints of the church of the Lamb, and upon the covenant people of the Lord, who were scattered upon all the face of the earth; and they were armed with righteousness and with the power of God in great glory. (1 Nephi 14:12–14.)

The Gospel Shall Roll Forth

My father possessed a vision of missionary service and the future growth of the Church. On more than one occasion, he made reference to a revelation given through the Prophet Joseph Smith in 1831, eighteen months after the organization of The Church of Jesus Christ of Latter-day Saints. It reads: "The keys of the kingdom of God are committed unto man on the earth, and from thence shall the gospel roll forth unto the ends of the earth, as the stone which is cut out of the mountain without hands shall roll forth, until it has filled the whole earth. . . . Wherefore, may the kingdom of God go forth, that the kingdom of heaven may come, that thou, O God, mayest be glorified in heaven so on earth, that thine enemies may be subdued; for thine is the honor, power and glory, forever and ever. Amen." (D&C 65:2, 6.)

I trusted my father. He was an honest man. Yet I questioned the prophecy of the stone rolling forth and filling the whole earth because Church membership was less than one million, the full-time missionary force was comparatively small, proselyting was restricted to just a handful of countries, and "Mormons" were regarded as members of a strange cult in the western United States. Notwithstanding all of this, my father assured me that the prophecy would be fulfilled in due time.

My father viewed things through eyes of faith. He believed that "the Gods watched those things which they had ordered until they obeyed" (Abraham 4:18). He envisioned a growing missionary force "armed with righteousness and with the power of God in great glory" (1 Nephi 14:14). He could foresee a time when Latter-day Saints and their way of life would gain greater respect among men and nations. He sensed a world hungering for the truths of the restored gospel.

Every Member a Missionary

I have often wondered what was in President David O. McKay's mind when he invited member participation in missionary service with the rallying cry, "Every member a missionary." He may have been thinking about this scripture: "I give unto you a commandment, that every man, both elder, priest, teacher, and also member, go to with his might, with the labor of his hands, to prepare and accomplish the things which I have commanded. And let your preaching be the warning voice, every man to his neighbor, in mildness and in meekness." (D&C 38:40–41.)

Whatever prompted President McKay to stir member interest in sharing the gospel, it is certain that he knew the potential power for good of one million member-missionaries, in addition to the relatively small corps of full-time missionaries. Perhaps he envisioned the following dramatic growth pattern of the Church:

- The Church required 117 years to reach a membership of one million (1830–1947).
- It required sixteen more years to reach a membership of two million (1947–1963).
- It required eight more years to reach a membership of three million (1963–1971).
- It required seven more years to reach a membership of four million (1971–1978).
- It required four more years to reach a membership of five million (1978–1982).
- It required four more years to reach a membership of six million (1982–1986).
- It required three more years to reach a membership of seven million (1986–1989).
- It required two and a half more years to reach a membership of eight million (1989–1991).
- It required three more years to reach a membership of nine million (1991–1994).
- The ten-million membership mark will likely be reached in 1996. (See *Deseret News 1995–96 Church Almanac* [Salt Lake City: Deseret News, 1994], pp. 418–20.)

"Lengthen Our Stride"

President Spencer W. Kimball was a visionary prophet with deep interest in missionary service. He had much to say about the future growth of the kingdom of God on earth. And he knew what had to be done to "lengthen the stride" of both members and missionaries. Note the thrilling insights in these declarations:

Every member knows of nonmembers he or she can refer to the missionaries. Every father, mother, and youth of this Church should share the gospel by giving a Book of Mormon, telling the account of the Prophet Joseph Smith, or inviting our acquaintances to a special meeting. If we are in tune, the Spirit of the Lord will speak to us and guide us to those with whom we should share the gospel. The Lord will help us if we will but listen. (Regional Representatives' Seminar, April 1975; quoted in Ezra Taft Benson, "President Kimball's Vision of Missionary Work," *Ensign*, July 1985, p. 11.)

In stake missionary work, I know a good man who with his family set their goal to bring into the Church a family a year. I believe it was about 14 years they have been doing this and they have brought about 14 families into the Church to their credit.

If half a million Church families would do likewise, that would mean a million and a half new members through the family each year.

We are not interested in numbers. They are secondary. We are interested in warning the nations of the world. I believe we have not scratched the surface. We are like the person who said, "Pull up the ladder; I'm aboard." . . .

In the [lobby of the Church Office Building] is a beautiful mural. . . . It shows the Lord and his Apostles on the Mount of Olives. I imagine his feet were weary and his body strained, but his spirit was alive and alert. He is giving the last instructions to his leaders who will carry on. Perhaps he is thinking: "Go with a faith like that of Moses, that the impossible can happen—the sea can open, the enemy pursuers can be stopped, the east wind can be controlled and the children of Israel can be given a new world, a new vision, a new opportunity." Perhaps he is thinking: "There are bushes aflame with God in every desert; if one can see and hear and understand, revelation is there." Perhaps he is saying: "There is a smooth stone in every shepherd's pouch and a sling in every hand and a faith in every heart, a true marksman David for every Goliath." Maybe he is thinking: "There is a Brigham Young with perception and faith and understanding for every wandering company of pioneers—a leader who will see them through to their eternal destination." Perhaps he was seeing many Wilford Woodruffs hollowing out little ponds and baptizing thousands of followers. He is saying, "Go ye into all the world and preach the gospel to every creature." Perhaps he is thinking of Yugoslavia and Iran and India and Greece and Czechoslovakia and Russia, that will come into being after his crucifixion and ascension, with closed doors which will need to be opened. Maybe he is thinking also of Rumania and Poland and China and Burma, which may need a burning bush and revelation, and maybe thinking of places where a Moses might strike his rod and cause water to flow. He *is* saying without all of the explanations of the hows and whys, "Go ye into all the world and preach the gospel to every creature." (Regional Representatives' Seminar, 3 October 1974.)

Concluding Word

The spirit and vision of missionary service go hand in hand. When one is touched by the Spirit, he wants to be up and doing—he desires to be an active participant in the process of saving souls. However, unless one catches a vision of what is and what can be, his efforts may be halfhearted or misdirected. For example, a farmer clears the ground, tills the soil, and does all else to provide food for loved ones. But until he exercises faith and sees in his mind's eye ripened grain and bread on the table, he will not drop the seed into the ground with a sense of urgency. In a similar manner, a Latter-day Saint is loathe to share the gospel unless he feels the Spirit and gains glorious views of what the gospel of Jesus Christ can do in the lives of people.

At a seminar for new mission presidents and wives, President Thomas S. Monson stated: "Work without vision is drudgery. Vision without work is dreaming. Work coupled with vision is destiny." ("Keys to Successful Missionary Work," Provo, Utah, 23 June 1987.)

For the purposes of this book, I've made some slight changes in his words. In my experience, missionary service without the Spirit and vision is drudgery. Having the Spirit and vision without service is idle dreaming. And missionary service coupled with the Spirit and with vision is destiny.

I close this introductory statement by repeating an earnest appeal voiced by President Ezra Taft Benson. He taught: "Let us exhort each other to fulfill our missionary responsibility. Let us do it with love—not criticism. Let us do it with understanding—not berating. But let us do it, and do it with urgency. *Let us catch the vision and the inspiration of President Kimball.* We need to understand that member-missionary work is literally the key to the future growth of the Church and that we have covenanted with our Father in Heaven to do this work." ("President Kimball's Vision of Missionary Work," *Ensign*, July 1985, p. 11; emphasis added.)

1

MANKIND

"The Whole Human Family of Adam"

We know of no one in life who isn't an Important Person. We know of no man on the street (or in the gutter, for that matter) who isn't a child of God with the same rights and with the same relationship to his Father in heaven as all the rest of us have.

We know of no one, young or old, from infants to elderly individuals, whose past or whose potential we would want to appraise as being unimportant. We know of no one we might see in any public place—on subways or busses, or walking in shabby shoes—or any boy selling papers, or any abandoned urchin, who doesn't have an inestimable, unknown potential, here and hereafter. (Quoted in Richard L. Evans Jr., Richard L. Evans—The Man and the Message [Salt Lake City: Bookcraft, 1973], p. 304.)

The first M of missionary service is mankind. It applies to all of God's children irrespective of race, color, creed, or language. He who is the Father of all declared, "Know ye not that there are more nations than one? Know ye not that I, the Lord your God, have created all men, and that I remember those who are upon the isles of the sea; and that I rule in the heavens above and in the earth beneath; and I bring forth my word unto the children of men, yea, even upon all the nations of the earth?" (2 Nephi 29:7.)

Yes, the heart and soul of missionary service is a genuine love for all mankind, including a love for the woman on the street, the man in the gutter, and the abandoned urchin. Without this love, there is little inclination to share with others the truth and virtue Latter-day Saints possess. With this love, however, there is a willful, even anxious, desire to reach down, lift up, speak out, and do all within our power to bless the lives of men, women, and children. Missionary service is indeed a labor of love, and those who become active participants must see inherent goodness and potential in everyone. We must be willing "to give, not to take" and be eager "to serve, not to exploit" (Spencer W. Kimball, *Faith Precedes the Miracle* [Salt Lake City: Deseret Book Co., 1972], p. 157).

John the Apostle wrote: "If a man say, I love God, and hateth his brother, he is a liar: for he that loveth not his brother whom he hath seen, how can he love God whom he hath not seen? And this commandment have we from him, That he who loveth God love his brother also." (1 John 4:20–21.)

Love of God and love of all mankind are intertwined and inseparable. Affection for one is affection for the other; goodness extended to the Father's children is goodness extended to the Father. Any parent whose son or daughter has been helped by some generous person understands the virtue in these words of the Master: "Inasmuch as ye have done it unto one of the least of these my brethren, ye have done it unto me" (Matthew 25:40).

Moreover, love—love of God and one's fellowmen—is a distinguishing feature of Christ's disciples. Said the Savior: "A new commandment I give unto you, That ye love one another; as I have loved you, that ye also love one another. By this shall all men know that ye are my disciples, if ye have love one to another." (John 13:34–35.)

Those who engage in missionary service out of sincere love for others do two things simultaneously. They demonstrate their love of God, and they pay the price of Christian discipleship. "Wherefore," pled the prophet Mormon, ". . . pray unto the Father with all the energy of heart, that ye may be filled with this love, which he hath bestowed upon all who are true followers of his Son, Jesus Christ" (Moroni 7:48).

Terror on the Bridge

There are times when our love and concern for others lies dormant within us. It is during such times that we go merrily on our way chasing selfish desires and giving little heed to the people around us.

We excuse our brusqueness and neglect by saying that this is a dog-eat-dog world we live in and that we must look out for our own interests. But when we are faced with a threatening situation in which precious lives hang in the balance, an alarm seems to go off within us and we instinctively act to save ourselves and others. Such conditions are illustrated in the following story and newspaper account:

Years ago the Australian city of Hobart, Tasmania, was divided by a river channel. To unite the city, a bridge was constructed at great cost to span the river. When completed, the bridge accomplished its purpose, and all were pleased about its erection. However, in January 1975 a ship with tall masts sailed through the channel and severed the bridge. The following day a newspaper account was published under the headline "Terror on the Bridge Edge." It read in part as follows:

HOBART.—A man and his wife told today of their seconds of terror in a car hanging half over the collapsed span of the Tasman Bridge with a 50-metre drop to the water below.

Mr. Frank Manley, 44, of Cambridge, his wife Sylvia, daughter Sharon, 16, and brother-in-law John Fitzgerald, 33, were driving along the mile-long bridge last night when suddenly there was no more roadway. Today, Mr. Manley, still shaking, told how his wife screamed: "Quick, there's no bridge."

Mr. Manley said: "That was it. It was too late. We were partly over the bridge—almost half the car was hanging. Sylvia scrambled out and told Sharon and John in the back seat to get out quickly. It's a two-door car and when I opened my door there was nothing—just a sheer drop. I scrambled out with my back pressed hard against the pillar of the car and eased myself back on to the crumbling roadway," Mr. Manley said.

Mrs. Manley said: "As soon as I got out I ran down the road to tell people to stop. I just ran. I didn't look back. I tried to stop this bloke in a yellow car. He was going too fast. He nearly ran me down. I screamed at him and he slammed into the back of a car beside us and pushed him over the edge so that car was hanging like ours. Then came a bus, I waved. He turned his wheel and just missed a car."

The man in the other car left teetering over the brink is Mr. Murray Ling, a Beelerive. He, his wife and two children were crossing the bridge when the lights went out. Mr. Ling said: "I knew something bad must have happened and I slowed down. I stopped three feet from the gap, I think. I got out and started waving and a car came through fast in another lane. He thumped into another car, flew past and dropped over the edge." (*Melbourne, Australia, Herald*, 6 January 1975, p. 1.)

I ask, Why did Mrs. Manley and Mr. Ling throw all caution to the wind on that fateful night and race toward the oncoming traffic shouting warnings to total strangers? Why did they place their own lives in jeopardy without measuring carefully the possible consequences of their heroic actions? I believe that they acted the way they did because the immortal spirits within them were awakened by the threat at hand and could not be restrained. They called out and provoked actions in behalf of kindred spirits who might have perished if others had remained in their automobiles and failed to open their mouths.

Brothers and Sisters All

We are the children of God—all of us. He is the Father of all spirits (see Hebrews 12:9). The spirit or breath of life within us was sired by God, and so was the spirit that inhabits our bodies. When we speak of the twin concepts of the Fatherhood of God and the brotherhood of man, we speak of spiritual ties of great significance.

Moreover, there are physical or mortal relationships not to be regarded lightly. Is not Adam our common ancestor or father? "In Hebrew *adam* is also a common noun, meaning man, or mankind" (Genesis 5:2, footnote A). Do we not belong to the whole human family of Adam? (See 2 Nephi 9:21.) And have we not been taught that we are our "brother's keeper?" (Genesis 4:9.)

Of a truth, there are inborn spiritual and physical ties between people everywhere. Such ties may hang rather loosely in our lives or even be taken for granted. But in moments of impending doom, such as when bridges come tumbling down, something stirs inside us and causes us to rise above selfish interests and throw lifelines to others.

God's Love for All Mankind

A number of years ago the First Presidency of The Church of Jesus Christ of Latter-day Saints issued a statement entitled "God's Love for All Mankind." It reads:

Based upon ancient and modern revelation, The Church of Jesus Christ of Latter-day Saints gladly teaches and declares the Christian doctrine that all men and women are brothers and sisters, not only by blood relationship from mortal progenitors, but also as literal spirit children of an Eternal Father.

The great religious leaders of the world such as Mohammed, Confucius, and the Reformers, as well as philosophers including Socrates, Plato, and others, received a portion of God's light. Moral truths were given to them by God to enlighten whole nations and to bring a higher level of understanding to individuals.

The Hebrew prophets prepared the way for the coming of Jesus Christ, the promised Messiah, who should provide salvation for all mankind who believe in the gospel.

Consistent with these truths, we believe that God has given and will give to all people sufficient knowledge to help them on their way to eternal salvation, either in this life or in the life to come.

We also declare that the gospel of Jesus Christ, restored to his Church in our day, provides the only way to a moral life of happiness and a fullness of joy forever. For those who have not received this gospel, the opportunity will come to them in the life hereafter if not in this life.

Our message therefore is one of special love and concern for the eternal welfare of all men and women, regardless of religious belief, race, or nationality, knowing that we are truly brothers and sisters because we are sons and daughters of the same Eternal Father. (Quoted in "I Have a Question," *Ensign*, January 1988, p. 47.)

There are those who wonder why the Latter-day Saints are so missionary-minded and so intent upon sharing their faith with others. Perhaps our efforts to share saving covenants and ordinances would be more appreciated if others understood that our love for all mankind emanates from our Father's love for all mankind, and if they understood that God's work and glory of bringing to pass the immortality and eternal life of man is also our work and glory (see Moses 1:39).

The Lord declared to a repentant Alma, "Marvel not that all mankind, yea, men and women, all nations, kindreds, tongues and people, must be born again; yea, born of God, changed from their carnal and fallen state, to a state of righteousness, being redeemed of God, becoming his sons and daughters; and thus they become new creatures; and unless they do this, they can in nowise inherit the kingdom of God" (Mosiah 27:25–26).

Each time I read the above statement and reflect upon missionary service, three personal experiences come to mind.

"God Sent You to Me"

A few years ago my wife and I were privileged to visit a small branch of members who lived on the island of Bahrain located off the coast of the Arabian Peninsula in the Persian Gulf. One morning as we took our daily walk, we explored a rural part of the island. We came upon an oasis-like housing development nestled in a grove of palm trees. Some homes were occupied; others were still under construction. All were very large and very beautiful. Our survey of the place was brief, and we soon began the long stroll back to the city.

All of a sudden, a dark-skinned Indian woman came running toward us, waving her hand and signaling for us to wait. We didn't know what was wrong, so we stopped and waited. Once at our side, and all out of breath, she asked if she could walk with us into the city. She explained that her taxi had failed to arrive at the appointed time and that she needed to go into town to purchase some needed medicine. She needed our protection because several local women had recently been attacked and molested by some thugs.

We were happy to oblige our unknown friend. In fact, we walked out of our way to make certain that she reached her destination safely. As we parted company, she bowed very low to us, shook our hands warmly, and said: "I prayed that you would come. God sent you to me!"

This declaration of faith by a total stranger of another color, race, and religion was thrilling to us. Obviously she was a believer who possessed a depth of love for and confidence in God that was extraordinary, much more than lip service.

That experience with the Indian woman in Bahrain and similar experiences with good people the world over have stamped in my mind these truths: "God is no respecter of persons: but in every nation he that feareth him, and worketh righteousness, is accepted with him" (Acts 10:34–35).

Moreover, "he inviteth them all to come unto him and partake of his goodness; and he denieth none that come unto him, black and white, bond and free, male and female; and he remembereth the heathen; and all are alike unto God, both Jew and Gentile" (2 Nephi 26:33).

How could it be otherwise as long as he is the Father of all spirits?

"Were You Praying Too?"

My second experience happened as I boarded a plane one day in Dallas, Texas. The airline representative announced to us that there would be open seating on that particular flight to Lubbock. I moved slowly down the aisle, looking for someone interesting to sit by.

I noticed a young woman seated by herself in the third row with an open Bible on her lap. I thought to myself, *Here is a God-fearing person; perhaps she will be interested in hearing my testimony.* "Do you mind if I fly with you to Lubbock?" I asked. She responded: "What good would it do if I objected? You have a valid ticket, don't you?" Then she smiled warmly and added, "Have a seat."

Once the airplane had gained its altitude, I initiated the conversation by saying, "You must enjoy reading the scriptures." This comment opened the floodgates of her faith. She shared with me her love of the Savior, her love for the word of God, and her love for the church with which she was affiliated. I was impressed by her sincerity and her enthusiasm for religion.

When she had finished her discussion, she was obligated to ask me the purpose of my travel. I proceeded to tell her that I was a mission president and that I was scheduled to speak in a church meeting that very evening. I also shared with her the story of the restoration of the gospel and the coming forth of the Book of Mormon. Both accounts intrigued her very much, causing her to agree that she would receive the missionaries I promised to send.

Midway through the flight, the pilot informed us that there was a heavy fog hovering over Lubbock. He indicated that if the weather didn't change, we would be diverted to an alternate destination. The news disturbed me greatly because I didn't want to miss the important meeting scheduled for that evening. Of course, all the people on the plane groaned when the news was broadcast. I closed my eyes and silently prayed that the sky would clear, making the landing possible. A few minutes later the pilot spoke again and announced that the fog had lifted unexpectedly and that we would arrive as planned.

Everyone on the plane cheered at the good news. I turned to my traveling companion and said, "Now, that was a quick answer to a prayer!"

"Oh," she said, "were you praying too?"

To my dying day I will wonder whose faith and prayer worked the miracle—hers or mine? Probably our prayers were both heard and answered that day.

My conversation with the young lady brought to mind these words: "There are many yet on the earth among all sects, parties, and denominations . . . who are only kept from the truth because they know not where to find it" (D&C 123:12).

That encounter also reminded me that those who have accepted Christ and who have embraced the fulness of the restored gospel have the responsibility to "waste and wear out our lives in bringing to light all the hidden things of darkness, wherein we know them; and they are truly manifest from heaven" (D&C 123:13).

"Who Has Need of the Physician?"

My third experience: One weekend when I had no Church assignments, I decided to attend a sacrament service in a local ward. I took my seat in front on the stand and watched the people gather. A few of the people who came in I knew; most I did not.

Just moments before the meeting started, I saw two missionaries come in through a side door with a woman—a very worldly-looking woman. It was obvious that she was new to the group because she looked apprehensively from side to side and had to be guided to her seat. She was dressed in faded jeans and a tight sweater, and her face was heavily made up. Her dark and hardened countenance seemed to reflect a life of sin that was frightening to contemplate.

I couldn't help but wonder who would be successful in influencing the other—she the missionaries, or the missionaries her. Immediately following the service, I sought out one of the missionaries and spoke with him privately about the woman he and his companion had brought to church. My initial question was: "Elder, where did you meet that worldly woman?" My tone of voice was Pharisaic, inferring that he had brought to church someone who was unworthy of the privilege of worshiping with our group. The missionary bristled a little bit, stood his ground, and replied, "Elder Asay, who has need of the physician, the sick or the whole?" (See Matthew 9:9–13.)

Well, he had backed me into a corner. How could I question or refute what he and his good companion were attempting to do for someone who was spiritually sick and in desperate need of help from Christ, the Great Physician?

All I could say in return was: "Be careful! Make certain that she doesn't tempt or contaminate you."

Time passed, and I almost completely forgot the incident. But some months later I attended a fast and testimony meeting in the same chapel. The crowd was much the same as before; some I recognized, some I didn't. One woman entered alone, walked down the aisle, and seated herself near the front of the chapel. She sat quietly, meditated, and waited for the start of the meeting. She was dressed tastefully and her face reflected a special saintliness. In fact, she was beautiful. There was something familiar about her, but I couldn't be sure whether I had ever seen her before. No one in the congregation seemed to worship as intently as she did during the service. She seemed to sing and pray with all her heart.

It was a fast Sunday. The bishop bore his testimony and then invited others to bear theirs. The beautiful young woman was the first to respond. She stepped to the pulpit and began to speak. Among other things she tearfully told of how the missionaries had literally fished her out of the gutter, encouraged her to repent, and introduced her to members of the Church and to the fulness of the gospel. It was then that I realized she was the woman dressed in jeans that I had seen in church with the missionaries only a few weeks before. A miraculous transformation had taken place through the efforts of two dedicated missionaries who looked upon the woman not as she was but as she could become.

I have often wondered about that woman who forsook the ways of the world and embraced saving truths at the invitation of two caring and loving missionaries. Perhaps there was a time when she cried out as the Psalmist, "I looked on my right hand, and beheld, but there was no man that would know me: refuge failed me; no man cared for my soul" (Psalm 142:4). Perhaps there was a time when she pleaded:

> I wish that there were some wonderful place
> Called the Land of Beginning Again,
> Where all our mistakes and all our heartaches
> And all of our poor selfish grief
> Could be dropped like a shabby old coat at the door,
> And never be put on again.
> (Louisa Fletcher, "The Land of Beginning Again.")

There is a land of beginning again! This blessed land is the gospel of Jesus Christ—the gospel of repentance. Those errant souls who fall into the pit of sin and become fettered by feelings of remorse can find new hope and new life by accepting the invitation to "come unto Christ" (Moroni 10:32).

But someone who possesses a love for others must be willing and ready to share the divine invitation. Such sharing must be free of prejudice, parochialism, or paradox. It must be done by those who love all mankind, whether they be non-Christian, professed Christians, or gross sinners. It must be done by those who are judicious rather than judgmental, merciful rather than merciless, and loving rather than listless.

Unless such messengers see value in every individual they meet, it is questionable whether they will extend the divine invitation in an acceptable manner. If, however, they regard all men and women as their brothers and sisters—made "a little lower than the angels" (Psalm 8:4–5)—and as worthy members of "the whole human family of Adam" (Mormon 3:20), their message or entreaty will ring with sincerity and be accompanied by compelling power. The message of love is effective only when the messenger has his or her heart in it.

A Matter of Love

You will recall the occasion when a lawyer tempted the Savior by asking, "Master, which is the great commandment in the law? Jesus said unto him, Thou shalt love the Lord thy God with all thy heart, and with all thy soul, and with all thy mind. This is the first and great commandment. And the second is like unto it, Thou shalt love thy neighbour as thyself. On these two commandments hang all the law and the prophets." (Matthew 22:36–40.)

Other scriptural references remind us that to love God with all our hearts and to love our neighbor as ourself "is more than all whole burnt offerings and sacrifices" (Mark 12:33). Moreover, "love worketh no ill to his neighbour: therefore love is the fulfilling of the law" (Romans 13:10). If love of God and one's fellowmen fulfills the law and is regarded as more than burnt offerings and sacrifices, how can we possibly ignore the woman on the street, the man in the gutter, and the abandoned urchin when we have precious, saving truths to share?

Our feelings towards the world of mankind, generally, ought to be the same as Jesus manifested to them. He sought to promote their welfare, and our motto ought ever to be the same as his was—"Peace on earth and good will to men;" no matter who they are or what they are, we should seek to promote the happiness and welfare of all Adam's race. (John Taylor, in Journal of Discourses 14:188.)

2

MESSAGE

"Come unto Christ, . . .
and Partake of His Salvation"

We invite all men everywhere to read the Book of Mormon, to ponder in their hearts the message it contains, and then to ask God, the Eternal Father, in the name of Christ if the book is true. Those who pursue this course and ask in faith will gain a testimony of its truth and divinity by the power of the Holy Ghost. (See Moroni 10:3–5.)

Those who gain this divine witness from the Holy Spirit will also come to know by the same power that Jesus Christ is the Savior of the world, that Joseph Smith is his revelator and prophet in these last days, and that The Church of Jesus Christ of Latter-day Saints is the Lord's kingdom once again established on the earth, preparatory to the second coming of the Messiah. (Introduction to the Book of Mormon.)

The second M of missionary service is the message—a saving message from God to all mankind.

To Know God

We boldly declare to the world that God the Father and his Son Jesus Christ revealed themselves to the Prophet Joseph Smith in the spring of 1830. Such revelation came in answer to a humble prayer wherein a believing boy inquired as to which of all the sects or churches was right. Not only did he learn that they were all wrong, but he also learned about the true nature of God, thus dispelling mysteries that had troubled the minds of men for many centuries.

In one glorious experience—now referred to as the First Vision—Joseph Smith gained a sure knowledge of some basic and undergirding truths. Four of those basic truths are: (1) that the powers of darkness or Satan are real but can be overcome by the powers of God; (2) that a soul at this time is as precious unto God as in times past (see Alma 39:17); (3) that visions or revelations and answers to prayers are not things reserved for the past; (4) that God the Father and God the Son are two separate and distinct Personages who have a continuing interest in the affairs of men on the earth.

We do, therefore, declare to all truth seekers: "We believe in God, the Eternal Father, and in His Son, Jesus Christ, and in the Holy Ghost" (Articles of Faith 1:1). Yes, we believe in a loving Father in Heaven who is "the Father of spirits" (Hebrews 12:9) and in whose image man was made. Moreover, we believe that Jesus the Christ is the Only Begotten Son of God in the flesh and the Savior of the world. We also believe that the Holy Ghost, a personage of spirit, is the third member of the Godhead and is the primary messenger through whom the Father and the Son work in bringing to pass their purposes as pertaining to those who dwell upon this earth.

It must not be forgotten that in his great intercessory prayer, the Savior stated: "And this is life eternal, that they might know thee the only true God, and Jesus Christ, whom thou hast sent" (John 17:3).

More than once in the scriptures, the Lord refers to his servants as his friends. One reference reads: "I give unto you this commandment, that ye become *even as my friends* in days when I was with them, traveling to preach the gospel in my power" (D&C 84:77; emphasis added). Missionaries and members do, in fact, befriend the Lord by introducing him to others not as some fearsome or impersonal power but as a loving, kind, and benevolent Elder Brother who wants all Heavenly Father's children to come unto him.

The children of God who know the Lord have the responsibility and privilege of helping those who know him not. In doing so, it should be remembered that to know him is to love him, to love him is to keep his commandments, and to keep his commandments is to receive eternal life.

The Book of Life

I know of a rather prominent convert who became acquainted with the true and living God through the efforts of some fine young missionaries. She was asked: "Why did you agree to be baptized and become a member of The Church of Jesus Christ of Latter-day Saints?"

Her response: "My previous church affiliation provided me one chapter of the book of life. The minister and members of that church helped me to understand the purpose of mortality. However, your missionaries told me about a premortal and a post-earth life. With those two additional chapters, I now have the full book of life."

The message carried by missionaries and Church members does address those three important questions: Where did I come from? Why am I here? And where will I go after death?

For centuries men have speculated over scriptures such as: "Where wast thou when I laid the foundations of the earth? . . . When the morning stars sang together, and all the sons of God shouted for joy?" (Job 38:4, 7.) Or, "And there was war in heaven: Michael and his angels fought against the dragon; and the dragon fought and his angels, and prevailed not; neither was their place found any more in heaven" (Revelation 12:7–8). The full meaning of these and other references remained hidden until the restoration of the gospel of Jesus Christ. Line upon line, precept by precept, Joseph Smith received knowledge concerning a war in heaven, the foreordination of priesthood leaders or the "noble and great ones" (Abraham 3:22; see also Alma 13), and other equally essential doctrines. As a result, the light in the back room of our memories has grown brighter and brighter with each revelation received, and our views of the future have become more and more glorious.

Perhaps there was a time when men wondered about the real purpose of earth life. Such wondering was brought to a close by these illuminating words of Jehovah: "We will go down, for there is space there, and we will take of these materials, and we will make an earth whereon these may dwell; and we will prove them herewith, to see if they will do all things whatsoever the Lord their God shall command them" (Abraham 3:24–25). Hence, the two-fold purpose of life: (1) to receive a body of flesh and bones, and (2) to prove ourselves worthy of returning to the God who gave us life by making the most of this probationary state called life (see Alma 12:24). It is so very simple, yet so very profound!

Holy writ abounds with references to physical death, resurrection, a judgment day, eternal life, and all else that testifies of life beyond the grave. Jesus taught: "I am the resurrection, and the life: he that believeth in me, though he were dead, yet shall he live" (John 11:25). Who will ever forget Job's stirring declaration, "For I know that my redeemer liveth, and that he shall stand at the latter day upon the earth; and though after my skin worms destroy this body, yet in my flesh shall I see God" (Job 19:25–26). These are only two of many assurances gleaned from the scriptures that there is a life after death or a postmortal existence. There are many, many more.

Members and missionaries, all who believe in the true and living God, are privileged to share the book of life with members of the human family. Each chapter is exciting; each chapter is reassuring; and each chapter gives us purpose and direction for living. There is no other message quite so timely or compelling.

Four Questions

In my mind, the message carried into the world by members and missionaries begins with a knowledge of God, expands to include the three chapters in the book of life, and is focused upon "the great plan of salvation" (Alma 42:5). This plan is sometimes referred to as "the great plan of happiness" (Alma 42:8), "the plan of redemption" (Alma 42:11), and "the great plan of mercy" (Alma 42:31). When all of these expressions are bound into one, they constitute the gospel of Jesus Christ—a gospel that blossoms in answer to the following questions:

Does God have an avowed purpose?

It is written: "For behold, this is my work and my glory—to bring to pass the immortality and eternal life of man" (Moses 1:39). Immortality or victory over physical death is an accomplished fact. Eternal life or victory over spiritual death is the pressing issue of the moment. These two gifts of God are compared in the following chart:

Immortality	Focal Point: Christ's Atonement	Eternal Life
• It is to live forever in the resurrected state with body and spirit inseparably connected. • It is victory over physical death (see Alma 11: 42, 45). • It is a free gift that comes by grace alone without works on man's part. • It is a gift for all mankind. • It comes through Christ's resurrection. • It is universal salvation. • It is unconditional salvation.		• It is the kind of life that our Eternal Father lives; God's life is eternal life. • It is victory over spiritual death (see Alma 11: 40–41; 12:16–18). • It results from obedience to the laws and ordinances of the gospel. • It is a synergistic product of God's grace and man's good works. • It is promised only to the righteous, repentant, and obedient. • It is individual salvation. • It is conditional salvation.

Yes, God does have an avowed purpose. It is summarized beautifully by Jacob, who taught:

> Therefore, cheer up your hearts, and remember that ye are free to act for yourselves—to choose the way of everlasting death or the way of eternal life.
> Wherefore, my beloved brethren, reconcile yourselves to the will of God, and not to the will of the devil and the flesh; and remember, after ye are reconciled unto God, that it is only in and through the grace of God that ye are saved.
> Wherefore, may God raise you from death by the power of the resurrection, and also from everlasting death by the power of the atonement, that ye may be received into the eternal kingdom of God, that ye may praise him through grace divine. Amen. (2 Nephi 10:23–25.)

Does God have an avowed plan?

If God declared his purpose and failed to provide a plan whereby his purpose might be accomplished, one would wonder about the genuineness of his love for mankind and his all-wiseness. However, he has provided a way for the realization of his great and eternal purposes, for his means are not vague, nor are they crooked. This way is sketched as follows:

The Gospel of Jesus Christ:
The "Strait and Narrow Path Which Leads to Eternal Life"
(2 Nephi 31:18)

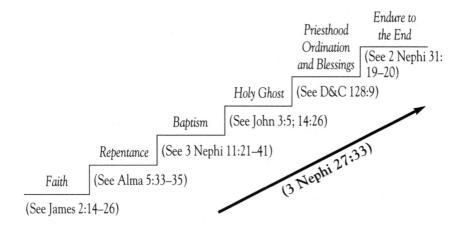

True messengers of the Lord Jesus Christ preach faith, repentance, baptism, and all the other truths that move people upward and onward. Their approach is direct: "Repent, and be baptized . . . for the remission of sins, and ye shall receive the gift of the Holy Ghost" (Acts 2:38). Their reliance is upon the word of God, believing that through the scriptures others will "come to the knowledge of their forefathers, and also to the knowledge of the gospel of their Redeemer . . . and the very points of his doctrine, *that they may know how to come unto him and be saved*" (1 Nephi 15:14; emphasis added).

If we are God's children as claimed, it follows that his purpose and plan should become our purpose and plan. Should not the children labor in support of their father?

Does God have an official organization or group of people through whom he works?

Yes, the organization is the Church, and his people are called Saints. Both the Church and the Saints are blessed through the leadership of duly called and authorized servants representing the Lord. Notice the purposes of the Church mentioned by Paul: "And he gave some, apostles; and some, prophets; and some, evangelists; and some, pastors and teachers; for the perfecting of the saints, for the work of the ministry, for the edifying of the body of Christ" (Ephesians 4:11–12).

Notice also the arrangement described in the following reference: "Now therefore ye are no more strangers and foreigners, but fellowcitizens with the saints, and of the household of God; and are built upon the foundation of the apostles and prophets, Jesus Christ himself being the chief corner stone; in whom all the building fitly framed together groweth unto an holy temple in the Lord" (Ephesians 2:19–21).

In furtherance of that grand and glorious objective of bringing to pass the immortality and eternal life of man, the mission of the Church and the Saints is threefold: To *proclaim* the gospel of Jesus Christ to every nation, kindred, tongue, and people; to *perfect* the Saints by preparing them to receive the ordinances of the gospel and gain exaltation; and to *redeem* the dead by performing vicarious ordinances of the gospel for those who have lived on the earth.

God does have an official organization and select group of people through whom he works to implement his plan and achieve his noble purposes. His instructions to the ancient Nephites still apply: "Now this is the commandment: Repent, all ye ends of the earth, and come unto me and be baptized in my name, that ye may be sanctified by the reception of the Holy Ghost, that ye may stand spotless before me at the last day. Verily, verily, I say unto you, this is my gospel; and ye know the things that ye must do in my church; for the works which ye have seen me do that shall ye also do; for that which ye have seen me do even that shall ye do." (3 Nephi 27:20–21.)

We solemnly declare to the world that the gospel of Jesus Christ has been restored to the earth through the instrumentality of Joseph Smith. The Church of Jesus Christ of Latter-day Saints is exactly what the name implies. It is Christ's church, and it is the same organization that existed in the primitive Church (see Articles of Faith 1:6).

By what power is the organization driven so that the plan may be implemented and the purpose realized?

As mentioned previously, the Prophet Joseph Smith was told not to join any of the sects of his day. Why? Because "they were all wrong; and the Personage who addressed me said that all their creeds were an abomination in his sight; that those professors were all corrupt; that: 'they draw near to me with their lips, but their hearts are far from me, they teach for doctrines the commandments of men, having a form of godliness, but they deny the power thereof'" (Joseph Smith—History 1:19).

False or assumed power has never saved anyone, nor will it ever. True and real priesthood power, however, is efficacious. As President Spencer W. Kimball said: "The priesthood is the power and authority of God delegated to man on earth to act in all things pertaining to the salvation of men. It is the means whereby the Lord acts through men to save souls. Without this priesthood power, men are lost." (*The Teachings of Spencer W. Kimball*, ed. Edward L. Kimball [Salt Lake City: Bookcraft, 1982], p. 494.)

Our testimony to the world is that God does perform his work on earth through men who are endowed with priesthood power—a power received by way of an oath and covenant. It is through the priesthood that the powers of godliness are manifested and worthy participants become saviors on Mount Zion and saviors of men (see Obadiah 1:21; D&C 103:9–10).

Gospel Perspective—an Analogy

The four questions related to the great plan of salvation constitute a gospel perspective. This perspective related to purpose, plan, people and power is understood more clearly by drawing the following analogy:

1. God's *purpose* may be likened to a *desired destination*—a place or state of being that we all want to reach.
2. God's *plan* may be likened to a *road map*—a map which, if followed, will lead us up the strait and narrow way to our desired destination.
3. God's *people* or church may be likened to a *vehicle* or a means of transportation used in carrying the Saints along the proper course to the desired destination.
4. God's *power* or priesthood may be likened to the *petrol or gasoline* used to propel the people and the Church forward along the approved route leading to the ultimate destination, even eternal life.

Perhaps the analogy drawn is an oversimplification of something very sacred and wonderful. But if these truths are not clearly understood, few members and missionaries will have the desire to share the message of the restored gospel and kingdom of God established on the earth.

Concluding Word

According to Elder Bruce R. McConkie, the issue in the meridian of time was, Did Christ rise from the dead? If he did not, he was an imposter. If he did, then he was all that he said he was, even the Savior of all mankind, and the religion of the ancient Saints had saving power. (See "Our Belief in Christ," *Improvement Era*, December 1970, p. 114.)

Centuries have come and gone since the Savior's birth, death, and resurrection. Evidences of his mortal ministry and victory over the grave have increased with the passage of time. His recorded words and works attest that he really was and still is the Son of God. So the issue surrounding his divinity is moot.

The issue of our day and time is: Was Joseph Smith a true prophet? Did he really see the Father and the Son in vision? If he did not, then he was the fraud of all frauds. If he did, then the religion of the Latter-day Saints has saving power.

Humbly but boldly, Church members and missionaries declare to the world "that Jesus Christ is the Savior of the world, that Joseph Smith is his revelator and prophet in these last days, and that The Church of Jesus Christ of Latter-day Saints is the Lord's kingdom once again established on the earth" (Introduction to the Book of Mormon). It is, therefore, the privilege of all true believers to proclaim this wonderful message and invite all to "come unto Christ, and be perfected in him, and deny yourselves of all ungodliness; and if ye shall deny yourselves of all ungodliness, and love God with all your might, mind and strength, then is his grace sufficient for you, that by his grace ye may be perfect in Christ; and if by the grace of God ye are perfect in Christ, ye can in nowise deny the power of God" (Moroni 10:32).

The Church of Jesus Christ of Latter-day Saints . . . claims to be a bold, prophetic, and inspired Church built upon the rock of revelation. It calls upon man to cooperate with God in his avowed purpose to bring to pass the immortality and eternal life of man. This is a divine partnership and is available to all. It gives added meaning to the term "the brotherhood of man." It is not simply a philosophy of life; it is a divine plan or blueprint of life—preexistent life, mortal life, and postmortal life. (Hugh B. Brown, in Conference Report, April 1969, p. 51.)

3

MEMBERS

"Every Member a Missionary"

In our preexistent state, . . . we made a certain agreement with the Almighty. . . . We agreed . . . to be not only saviors for ourselves but measurably, saviors for the whole human family. We went into a partnership with the Lord. The working out of the plan became then not merely the Father's work, and the Savior's work, but also our work. (John A. Widtsoe, "The Worth of Souls," Utah Genealogical and Historical Magazine, October 1934, p. 189.)

The third M of missionary service is the members—those who constitute a "cloud of witnesses" (Hebrews 12:1) and who may become multiplying factors in building the kingdom of God on the earth.

A Model of Righteousness

At a conference I heard a recent convert to the Church say, while pointing to the stake president sitting nearby: "I am a member of the Church today because this man is a model of righteousness." He explained that the stake president was one of the first men he met after being transferred to his company's home office. During his first days on the job, he mingled with a number of talented business executives; however, it didn't take him long to conclude that the stake president was the most honest, most positive, and most pleasing individual in the group.

One day the convert asked his coworker why he lived such a circumspect life and why he seemed to be a cut above the rest. The response was: "If there is anything distinctive about me, it is my faith—my commitment to the gospel of Jesus Christ." Then the stake president added: "Would you like to know more about my beliefs and way of life?"

The invitation was accepted, and the lives of a young man and several family members were changed. All grew to love the one who shared with them precious truths about God and the plan of salvation and other information that constitutes the foundation of a purposeful and happy life. In the process, the stake president provided saving services and advanced the Savior's work by helping to bring one more family into the kingdom of God.

Scriptural Foundations

Even a casual review of the scriptures reminds us that those who have received the gospel have the responsibility and opportunity to share it with others. Following are but a few references worthy of consideration.

An Expectation

In his Sermon on the Mount, Jesus preached: "Ye are the salt of the earth. . . . Ye are the light of the world. . . . Let your light so shine before men, that they may see your good works, and glorify your Father which is in heaven." (Matthew 5:13–14, 16.)

A modern version of this commission reads: "For they were set to be a light unto the world, and to be the saviors of men; and inasmuch as they are not the saviors of men, they are as salt that has lost its savor, and is thenceforth good for nothing but to be cast out and trodden under foot of men" (D&C 103:9–10).

There is a saying that where much is given, much is expected (see Luke 12:48; D&C 82:3). A related statement is "That which we willingly share, we keep; and that which we selfishly keep to ourselves, we lose" ("Status Report on Missionary Work," *Ensign*, October 1977, p. 11). These truisms certainly apply to those who have been privileged to hear and accept the fulness of the gospel of Jesus Christ. He who expects his followers to become perfect, "even as your Father which is in heaven is perfect" (Matthew 5:48), also expects them to be the salt of the earth, the light of the world, and saviors of men.

True believers, however, cannot share or give away that which they do not already possess. For instance, the sharing of a testimony is merely lip service unless it is an expression of faith that surges from the depths of one's soul. A casual act of kindness has its merits, but when that act is motivated by love and genuine concern for others, it becomes Christian service—service that blesses the receiver and sanctifies the giver.

When one considers thoughtfully the blessings associated with sharing the gospel, one understands the need to fulfill divine expectations.

A Commandment

A modern revelation includes this instruction: "I give unto you a commandment, that every man, both elder, priest, teacher, and also member, go to with his might, with the labor of his hands, to prepare and accomplish the things which I have commanded. And let your preaching be the warning voice, every man to his neighbor, in mildness and in meekness." (D&C 38:40–41.)

I have wondered over the years whether this scripture inspired President David O. McKay to declare: "Every member a missionary" (in Conference Report, April 1959, p. 122). The words "every man," "also member," and "every man to his neighbor" are all-inclusive. No member of the Church, it seems, is exempt from the requirement to share the restored gospel. All are expected to labor, preach, and warn others. A prophet coined the phrase "Every member a missionary," but have the members adopted the practice? This is the real issue.

There is a vast difference between an idle suggestion and a commandment. One is optional, and the other is not. One implies action if time is available and the inclination is strong enough. The other requires action whatever the circumstance, because the Lord provides "means whereby they can accomplish the thing which he has commanded them" (1 Nephi 17:3). Therefore, it is important that members of the Church remember that it is a commandment, not a suggestion, that they become active participants in missionary service.

Sometimes Church members feel overwhelmed with the assignment to share the restored gospel of Jesus Christ with the world. "We are so few in numbers," they say, "and there are so many millions among the nations." They wonder whether the work can be done. With such doubters in mind, Elder Boyd K. Packer wrote: "We are commanded to preach the gospel to all the living. . . . We see no way to accomplish this task in our lifetime. Many refuse to listen, some turn away, others resent and even persecute us. Nevertheless we are not released from the assignment to try. We are to do the best we can. If we do, the honest in heart can be found and sifted out of the world." (*The Holy Temple* [Salt Lake City: Bookcraft, 1980], p. 211.)

A Baptismal Commitment and Covenant

At the Waters of Mormon, Alma taught his humble followers the meaning and significance of baptism. He cited to his listeners a number of commitments made by those who submit to baptism and become members of the Church. Among other things, he emphasized the need for baptismal candidates to demonstrate a willingness "to stand as witnesses of God at *all times* and in *all things*, and in *all places* that ye may be in." (See Mosiah 18:8–11; emphasis added.)

I emphasize the "all-ness" of the baptismal commitment. Witnessing of God is not confined to a specific time, place, or circumstance. It is not something to be done once and then forgotten. It is not something to be reserved for a select few. It is not something to be jealously hoarded. Those who enter the Church through the waters of baptism covenant to do what Nephi declared: "For we labor diligently to write, to persuade our children, and also our brethren, to believe in Christ, and to be reconciled to God; for we know that it is by grace that we are saved, after all we can do. . . . And we talk of Christ, we rejoice in Christ, we preach of Christ, we prophesy of Christ, and we write according to our prophecies, that our children may know to what source they may look for a remission of their sins." (2 Nephi 25:23, 26.)

An Imperative Duty

In Liberty Jail, the Prophet Joseph Smith set forth the duty of Church members in relation to those who had persecuted them so badly. Three times the expression "imperative duty" is used in the instructions given. The third use of the expression seems to carry missionary connotations. It reads: "And also it is an imperative duty that we owe to all the rising generation, and to all the pure in heart—for there are many yet on the earth among all sects, parties, and denominations, who are blinded by the subtle craftiness of men, whereby they lie in wait to deceive, and who are only kept from the truth because they know not where to find it—therefore, that we should waste and wear out our lives in bringing to light all the hidden things of darkness, wherein we know them; and they are truly manifest from heaven" (D&C 123:11–13).

While it is true that Church members were counseled to publish the facts pertaining to their persecutions and to overcome the falsehoods circulated about their faith, it is also true that they were obligated to share the truth with those who knew not where to find it. Such action was not to be approached casually but as an urgent and compelling duty. Hence the concluding reminder: "For there is much which lieth in futurity, pertaining to the saints, which depends upon these things. . . . Therefore . . . let us cheerfully do all things that lie in our power." (D&C 123:15, 17.)

A Warning

"Behold," said the Lord, "I sent you out to testify and warn the people, and it becometh every man who hath been warned to warn his neighbor. Therefore, they are left without excuse, and their sins are upon their own heads." (D&C 88:81–82; see also Ezekiel 33:6–9.)

The above warning is reminiscent of the warnings given to ancient Israel. In one instance the watchmen were commanded to open their mouths and "to warn the wicked from his wicked way, to save his life." It was emphasized that if the warning were not given, and the man died in his iniquity, the watchman would be held accountable. (See Ezekiel 3:17–21, 27.)

In the other instance the "shepherds of Israel" were sorely chastised because they fed and clothed themselves but neglected to reach out to the scattered sheep. The indictment against the people of the Lord was as follows: "My flock was scattered upon all the face of the earth, and none did search or seek after them." The Lord's response and resolve was: "I, even I, will both search my sheep, and seek them out." (See Ezekiel 34:1–11.)

It is crystal clear that members of the Church are expected to serve as God's watchmen and shepherds. If they don't raise the warning voice, who will? If they don't seek out the scattered and feed them living waters and nourishing truths, who will?

Nearly a century ago Orson F. Whitney made this timeless statement: "The obligation of saving souls rests upon every man and woman in this Church—if not with equal weight, at least proportionately, according to their strength, their time, their opportunities, their abilities; and they cannot get out from under this responsibility on the plea that it belongs only to such and such persons. Did not the Lord say, through Joseph the Seer, at the beginning of this work, 'Behold, it is a day of warning, and not of many words: Therefore, let every soul that is warned, warn its neighbor'?" (In Conference Report, October 1913, p. 99.)

A Thing of Most Worth

John and Peter Whitmer wanted to know that which would be of most worth to them. Both were told: "I say unto you, that the thing which will be of the most worth unto you will be to declare repentance unto this people, that you may bring souls unto me, that you may rest with them in the kingdom of my Father" (D&C 15:6).

This scripture, along with the teachings of modern prophets, verifies two related facts: (1) our salvation is intertwined with the salvation of others, and (2) every member of the Church should be a missionary or a savior of men (see D&C 103:9–10). It also brings to mind the words of the poet John Greenleaf Whittier: "Heaven's gates are closed to he who comes alone; save thou a soul and save thine own" ("The Two Rabbins," *The Complete Poetical Works of Whittier* [Boston: Houghton Mifflin Co., 1894], pp. 91–92; see also 1 Timothy 4:16).

I have used six references which constitute a scriptural foundation for member participation in missionary service. Many other references could be cited. Let it be understood by all Saints that sharing the gospel with others is—

- An expectation
- A commandment
- A baptismal commitment and covenant
- An imperative duty
- A warning
- A thing of most worth

The How-To

I have a thesis that the spirit of missionary service grows as one becomes more and more involved in reaching out to others. One's desire to open his or her mouth or to extend the hand of friendship to another person may be weak or tentative to begin with. But as one engages in a gospel-sharing activity, however insignificant it may seem, a desire to do more bubbles up within one's heart. This is especially true if one's efforts result in the slightest measure of success. As the participation increases from general to more specific actions, the missionary spirit grows stronger and stronger.

My thesis is illustrated in the checklist included here, entitled "How Am I Doing as a Member Missionary?" You will notice that at the bottom of the chart the missionary spirit is weak or even asleep.

1. *Live:* The missionary spirit stirs and grows when one begins to live the commandments and model the gospel of Jesus Christ. Keep in mind that President Spencer W. Kimball said: "No greater service can be given to the missionary calling of the Church than to exemplify positive Christian virtues in our lives" (in Conference Report, October 1978, p. 7). Moreover, the Apostle Paul advised Timothy: "Be thou an example of the believers, in word, in conversation, in charity, in spirit, in faith, in purity" (1 Timothy 4:12).

The first chapter in many conversion stories begins with the words, "I met a Church member who was a model of righteousness." We must give credit to those who consciously strive to live and practice pure religion. They are performing a missionary service worthy of recognition. Consider the following letter:

> Dear Bill,
>
> I'm sure this letter comes as quite a surprise, as we haven't seen each other in six months. I'm writing to give you some very exciting news. I was baptized a member of the Church last Saturday night. I'm sure that comes as quite a shock to you, as you knew the type of life I led and the troubles I was in. Well, my life sure has changed for the good. And I wanted to tell you that you had a big part in it. You may not realize it, but your example played a big part in my conversion. While I never said anything, and you probably never knew, I had been watching you very closely, to see if you really lived your religion. And you did. *Your example provided for me the strength I needed to change.* After I moved away, I often thought of you and the life you

A Self-Evaluation:
How Am I Doing as a Member Missionary?

Use this self-evaluation form to assess your own involvement in sharing the gospel. Please note that the six categories of missionary activity proceed upward from general actions to more specific and involved actions. This is done with the assumption that the spirit of missionary service grows as one becomes more and more involved in reaching out to others.

Strong

Spirit of Missionary Service

(See Mosiah 28:3–4; Alma 29:1–2, 31:34–35; Ether 12:2–3.)

Weak

☐ 6. *Serve:* I am actively serving as a member-missionary by friendshipping non-member friends and families.
  • Prayerfully select a nonmember friend or family.
  • Plan and conduct friendshipping activities to interest them in the gospel.
  • Invite them to learn more about the Church and to participate in Church activities.
  • Refer them to the missionaries and assist in the conversion process.
  • Continue friendshipping those who are not yet ready, and continue fellowshipping those who become members of the Church.

☐ 5. *Testify:* I bear my testimony daily.
  • "Nevertheless, ye are blessed, for the testimony which ye have borne is *recorded in heaven for the angels to look upon;* and they rejoice over you, and *your sins are forgiven you*" (D&C 62:3; emphasis added).

☐ 4. *Prepare:* I am preparing myself and my family members to be missionaries.
  • Prepare for and serve a full-time mission upon retirement.
  • Prepare and send sons (and daughters if they so choose) on full-time missions.

☐ 3. *Send:* I am sending money, copies of the Book of Mormon, magazine subscriptions, golden referrals, and other things in support of the missionary cause.
  • Send contributions to the Church's general missionary fund (see D&C 66:6; 63:40–46).
  • Send copies of the Book of Mormon to nonmember friends.
  • Send Church magazine subscriptions to nonmember friends.
  • Send names and addresses of friends to the missionaries.

☐ 2. *Pray:* I pray that the doors to nations will open and that the hearts of men will soften.
  • "Nevertheless the children of God were commanded that they should gather themselves together oft, and join in fasting and mighty prayer in behalf of the welfare of the souls of those who knew not God" (Alma 6:6).
  • "We . . . hope that all people—parents, youth, children—will join in a serious, continuous petition to the Lord to open the gates of the nations and soften the hearts of the kings and the rulers to the end that missionaries may enter all the lands and teach the gospel" (Spencer W. Kimball, *The Teachings of Spencer W. Kimball,* ed. Edward L. Kimball [Salt Lake City: Bookcraft, 1982], p. 586).

☐ 1. *Live:* I am living the commandments and modeling the gospel of Jesus Christ.
  • "Be thou an example of the believers, in word, in conversation, in charity, in spirit, in faith, in purity" (1 Timothy 4:12; see also D&C 103:9–10).
  • "No greater service can be given to the missionary calling of the Church than to exemplify positive Christian virtues in our lives" (Spencer W. Kimball, in Conference Report, October 1978, p. 7).

led. Because you made the gospel come alive in your life, you made it possible for me to see it in action. Thanks for the help you probably didn't even know you were giving.

Love,

Hal

(*Seek to Obtain My Word: Melchizedek Priesthood Personal Study Guide 1989*, pp. 206–7; emphasis added.)

But is living the gospel enough and the desired end of our missionary activity? The obvious answer is no. We can and must do more!

2. *Pray:* A step up the involvement scale is to pray that the doors to nations will open and the hearts of men will soften so that the gospel may be preached and received. There was an instance when "the children of God were commanded that they should gather themselves together oft, and join in fasting and mighty prayer in behalf of the welfare of the souls of those who knew not God" (Alma 6:6). This commandment was echoed by President Spencer W. Kimball years ago: "We . . . hope that all people—parents, youth, children—will join in a serious continuous petition to the Lord to open the gates of the nations and soften the hearts of the kings and the rulers to the end that missionaries may enter all the lands and teach the gospel" (*The Teachings of Spencer W. Kimball* [Salt Lake City: Bookcraft, 1982], p. 586).

The preaching of the gospel of Jesus Christ and the conversion of people young or old is not mortals' work alone. It is God's work, and his spirit dwells among those who are honestly invested in it, whether they be preachers or humble hearers of the word (see Moses 1:39). Therefore, members of the Church are expected to do all within their power to advance the cause of righteousness and appeal to God in mighty prayer that he will not only find their efforts acceptable but crown their efforts with divine manifestations. Like one member-missionary observed: "I do all that I can possibly do before placing the matter into the hands of the Lord and trusting that he will do the rest."

I have the conviction that many miracles have occurred in times past and that many are now occurring as Church members share the gospel with others. The doors to nations are opening; walls of prejudice are tumbling down; and the once-stony hearts of next-door neighbors are softening. Why is all of this happening? I believe that the continuous appeals voiced by faithful Saints are being heard and answered by a loving God.

3. *Send:* Another step up the missionary involvement scale is to send materials that will advance the missionary cause—something that any timid soul can do. Send contributions to the Church's general missionary fund. These monies will enable others in underdeveloped countries to serve in missionary callings. Send copies of the Book of Mormon to nonmember friends. The book will teach and convert as it is read and prayed about. Send Church magazine subscriptions to truth-seeking friends. Many people hunger for wholesome reading materials, especially materials that include messages from living prophets. Send names and addresses of friends to the missionaries; it is, however, important that you obtain permission from your friends to submit their names as referrals. Send Tabernacle Choir tapes, Church videos, and other audiovisual items to interested friends. Many times these professional presentations will provide spiritual experiences that lead to conversion.

Send, send, send! Each of us has a circle of acquaintances. Moreover, many of us travel and enjoy brief visits with others on airplanes, on trains, on buses, and in public places. Oftentimes, these brief visits lead to discussions of religion. Why not follow up these brief visits and conversations with a note and enclosure such as a tape or book. Each item you send to represent your faith, if handled discreetly, carries the messages "I care about you"; "I'm interested in your welfare"; "I want to share with you something very precious." This is especially true of referrals.

4. *Prepare:* Still another step up the missionary involvement scale is to prepare. Every home should be a missionary training center, wherein parents and children are constantly strengthening the desire to serve and developing the abilities to share the gospel effectively.

Some years ago, President Spencer W. Kimball gave this inspired instruction:

> No person who has been converted to the gospel should shirk his responsibility to teach the truth to others. This is our privilege. This is our duty. This is a command from the Lord. . . .
>
> I was asked a few years ago, "Should every young man who is a member of the Church fill a mission?" And I responded with the answer the Lord has given: "Yes, every worthy young man should fill a

mission." The Lord expects it of him. And if he is not now worthy to fill a mission, then he should start at once to qualify himself. . . .

Someone might also ask, "Should every young woman, should every father and mother, should every member of the Church serve a mission?" Again, the Lord has given the answer: Yes, every man, woman, and child—every young person and every little boy and girl—should serve a mission. This does not mean that they must serve abroad or even be formally called and set apart as full-time missionaries. But it does mean that each of us is responsible to bear witness of the gospel truths that we have been given. We all have relatives, neighbors, friends, and fellow workmen, and it is our responsibility to pass the truths of the gospel on to them, by example as well as by precept. ("It Becometh Every Man," *Ensign*, October 1977, p. 11.)

Every home should be a center of strength and the hub of many missionary activities. It should be a place where young men (and young women who so desire) are preparing to serve full-time missions. It should be a place where parents are planning and preparing to serve missions after retirement. And it should be a place open to cottage meetings, community service, and other activities intended to share virtue and truth with others.

5. *Testify*: The fifth step up the scale of involvement, one that expands dramatically the missionary spirit, is to testify.

The story is told of one Church leader who asked a group of men: "Do you bear your testimonies each day?" Most admitted that they tried but were not always successful in doing so. The leader responded: "I don't try. I do! I do because of something the Lord said." He proceeded to read the following verse of scripture: "Nevertheless, ye are blessed, for the testimony which ye have borne is recorded in heaven for the angels to look upon; and they rejoice over you, and your sins are forgiven you" (D&C 62:3).

After a brief pause, he continued: "I want my testimony recorded in heaven. I want angels to look over me. You may not have as many sins as I do, but I want my sins forgiven."

In his epistle to the Hebrews, Paul the Apostle wrote: "Wherefore seeing we also are compassed about with *so great a cloud of witnesses*, let us lay aside every weight, and the sin which doth so easily beset us, and let us run with patience the race that is set before us, looking unto Jesus the author and finisher of our faith" (Hebrews 12:1–2; emphasis added).

If each member of the Church was looking for opportunities to bear his testimony on a daily basis, what a cloud of witnesses would form over our communities! This cloud would rain goodness upon people and bring about a cleansing that could not be achieved in any other way.

One caution: Precious declarations of faith should not be shared indiscriminately. Pearls should not be cast before swine. Something as sacred as one's testimony should not be voiced so frequently that it becomes a trite statement. However, I am convinced that we should and can preach "the word by the way" and find proper opportunities to testify, if we are prayerful and follow the promptings of the Holy Spirit (see D&C 52:9–27).

6. *Serve:* At the very apex of the missionary involvement scale is to serve—serve as member-missionaries. It is good to live, pray, send, prepare, testify, and do other things that cause people to act more righteously. Each action is virtuous and will bolster missionary service in any part of the world. However, all of these actions should not be regarded as the end of your contribution to the missionary effort. Rather, each should be regarded as a stepping-stone toward a stronger spirit and more productive involvement in sharing the gospel of Jesus Christ.

When a family (1) prayerfully selects a friend or family to work with, (2) plans and conducts friendshipping activities to interest them in the gospel, (3) invites them to learn more about the Church and to participate in Church activities, (4) refers them to the missionaries and assists in the conversion process, and (5) continues friendshipping those who are not yet ready to accept the gospel and fellowshipping those who become members of the Church, then they are serving as real member-missionaries.

Someone searched his own soul by asking: "What kind of church would this be if all the members were just like me?" Let me restate the question to fit this discussion: "What kind of a missionary church would this be if all the members were missionaries just like me?" It would be a more wonderful church and a stronger organization if every member understood and fulfilled his duty to preach the gospel by precept and example.

Why Has It Taken Me So Long?

Several years ago, I presided over a stake conference in the western part of the United States. The assigned theme for the Saturday evening session was missionary service. Some speakers talked about scriptural foundations for the work. Others spoke about ways and means of accomplishing the work and claiming the promised blessings. I felt prompted to encourage the members to be not only hearers but also doers of the word. Therefore, I challenged them to invite a nonmember friend to attend Church with them on Sunday morning.

More than a few accepted my challenge and brought friends with them to the worship service. Before the meeting started, one woman went out of her way to introduce her friend to me. Among other things she said: "Elder Asay, this is my very best friend. We have known each other for twenty years. But this is the first time that she has ever attended one of our meetings."

I thanked both women for coming to the conference, and I expressed my hope that the nonmember would enjoy her first experience in a Latter-day Saint gathering.

Throughout the meeting I carefully watched the nonmember. At first she appeared to be self-conscious and ill at ease. Later on she became absorbed in the proceedings and intrigued by the music and spoken word.

Immediately following the closing prayer, the nonmember friend rushed to the pulpit, leaving the member standing by herself and wondering what was happening, and said to me: "I have never heard such beautiful teachings. I have never felt this way before. Please tell me, why has it taken me all these years to find the truth?"

I could have pointed an accusing finger at her member friend who had waited twenty years to invite her to church. But I didn't. I simply assured her that she had found the truth and invited her to respond to her innermost feelings by receiving the missionaries and joining the Church. And she did so in a relatively short time.

"If the Good Will Lock Themselves Up . . ."

There is an interesting exchange between a perceptive woman and a prospective monk in one of Sir Arthur Conan Doyle's stories. The conversation proceeds as follows:

"God help me! I am the weakest of the weak," groaned Alleyne. "I pray that I may have more strength."

"And to what end?" she asked sharply. "If you are, as I understand, to shut yourself forever in your cell within the four walls of the abbey, then of what use would it be were your prayer to be answered?"

"The use of my own salvation."

She turned from him with a pretty shrug and wave. "Is that all?" she said. "Then you are no better than Father Christopher and the rest of them. Your own, your own, even your own! My father is the king's man, and when he rides into the press of fight he is not thinking ever of the saving of his own poor body; he recks little enough if he leave it on the field. Why then should you, who are soldiers of the Spirit, be ever moping or hiding in cell or in cave, with minds full of your own concerns, while the world, which you should be mending, is going on its way, and neither sees nor hears you? Were ye all as thoughtless of your own souls as the soldier is of his body, ye would be of more avail to the souls of others."

"There is sooth in what you say, lady," Alleyne answered; "and yet I scarce can see what you would have the clergy and the church to do."

"I would have them live as others and do men's work in the world, preaching by their lives rather than their words. I would have them come forth from their lonely places, mix with the borel folks, feel the pains and the pleasures, the cares and the rewards, the temptings and the stirrings of the common people. Let them toil and swinken, and labor, and plough the land, and take wives to themselves—"

"Alas! alas!" cried Alleyne aghast, "you have surely sucked this poison from the man Wicliffe, of whom I have heard such evil things."

"Nay, I know him not. I have learned it by looking from my own chamber window and marking these poor monks of the priory, their weary life, their profitless round. I have asked myself if the best which can be done with virtue is to shut it within high walls as though it were some savage creature. If the good will lock themselves up, and if the wicked will still wander free, then alas for the world!" (*The White Company*, quoted in Carlos E. Asay, *In the Lord's Service* [Salt Lake City: Deseret Book Co., 1990], pp. 41–42.)

Why was the young lady in the story displeased with the young man Alleyne? She assumed that he would one day return to the monastery, close himself away from the world, and become consumed with his own salvation. Such action she judged to be very selfish, especially for one who was spiritually inclined.

Why was the young lady critical of Father Christopher and the other men of the cloth? She referred to them as "soldiers of the Spirit," yet their minds were full of their own concerns and they were hiding in cell or cave and preaching by their words alone. In the meantime, the world around them was falling apart because they did not make themselves available to sinners.

What kind of a religious leader did the young lady desire? She wanted one who would mix with the rural folks, toil and sweat with the common people, and share the pains and pleasures of friends.

What did she accuse the monks of doing with virtue? She accused them of shutting it up within the walls of the abbey as if it were a savage creature. Then, her stinging conclusion: "If the good will lock themselves up, and if the wicked will still wander free, then alas for the world!"

Members of the Church are expected to be good soldiers of Jesus Christ or soldiers of the Spirit (see 2 Timothy 2:3). They should be models of moral excellence and righteousness. Their virtue can be an effective power to produce goodness in the lives of associates, if they make themselves available to others. How tragic it is when testimonies are never expressed, when service is withheld, or when virtue of whatever form is allowed to shrivel up and die within one's soul!

We read of a time when wickedness among members was "a great stumbling-block to those who did not belong to the church; and thus the church began to fail in its progress" (Alma 4:10). Stumbling blocks are turned into stepping-stones when Church members willfully live, pray, send, prepare, testify, and serve with the salvation of all mankind planted in their minds and hearts.

"All of this means," said President Spencer W. Kimball, "that we cannot share the gospel with every nation, kindred, tongue, and people (using only full-time) missionaries (as wonderful as they are), but we must have several million more to help them. We must, therefore, involve the members of the Church more effectively in missionary work. *Member-missionary work is the key to the future growth of the Church.*" (Regional Representatives Seminar, October 1980; emphasis added.)

The full-time missionary force will increase as the Church grows in membership. You can count on it. Proselyting efforts will become more productive as training programs and supportive materials are per-fected to meet the demands of the day. Nonetheless, the real multiply-ing factors of missionary service are and always will be the members themselves. When their support and participation is rallied, the work will accelerate forward under the watchful eyes of prophets past and present and under the all-seeing eye of a pleased Lord who "knoweth all things from the beginning; wherefore, he prepareth a way to ac-complish all his works among the children of men; for behold, he hath all power unto the fulfilling of all his words" (1 Nephi 9:6).

In the discharge of this duty every member of the Church should be a missionary; not necessarily to go forth into the world, but to preach the gospel to our neighbors and friends who are not in the Church. Moreover, by our example and our faithfulness to every commandment the Lord has given us to show our friends and the strangers within our gates the way to eternal life through our actions as well as through our words, that is, to be humble missionaries and advocates of the truth in our daily acts and conver-sations. (Joseph Fielding Smith, Answers to Gospel Questions, 5 vols. [Salt Lake City: Deseret Book Co., 1963], 4:55.)

4

FULL-TIME MISSIONARIES

"Missionaries to Match the Message"

And ye shall go forth in the power of my Spirit, preaching my gospel, two by two, in my name, lifting up your voices as with the sound of a trump, declaring my word like unto angels of God (D&C 42:6).

The fourth M of missionary service is the full-time missionaries—those who have received an unction from a living prophet to preach the gospel in all the world (see 1 John 2:20, 27).

Angelic Commission

Full-time missionaries, whether young or older, are given an angelic commission which requires them to—

Go Forth in the Power of the Spirit

The power of a missionary is not determined by his or her height, weight, or physical prowess. Nor is it determined by his or her smoothness of tongue or cleverness of mind. It is, however, determined by his or her receptivity to the Spirit and willingness to heed its promptings.

To go forth in the power of the Spirit means that a missionary must be taught and led by the Spirit and must teach by the Spirit. Therefore, the conscientious missionary courts the Holy Spirit every day of his mission. Such courting involves the exercise of faith, prayer, study, work, and righteous living. All of this is done with these promises in mind: (1) "The Spirit shall be given unto you by the prayer of faith" (D&C 42:14); and (2) "If ye will . . . receive the Holy Ghost, it will show unto you all things what ye should do" (2 Nephi 32:5). There is also the instruction that "if ye receive not the Spirit ye shall not teach" (D&C 42:14).

Missionaries must bear in mind that the Spirit or Holy Ghost enables a missionary to speak persuasively with "the tongue of angels" (2 Nephi 32:2). It serves as a conduit, if you will, through which the message passes from a missionary's heart to the heart of the listener. It is the power that converts.

The characteristic that most distinguishes true ministers of the gospel from people engaged in the works of the world is the presence and influence of the Holy Spirit. Said Brigham Young: "If those who are going to preach do not go with that faith that pertains to eternal life, and that spirit that is like a well of water, springing up into everlasting life, their labours will be vain. They may be the best theoretical theologians in the world—may be able to preach a Bible and a half in a sermon, to read history without a book, and understand all the dealings with men from the days of Adam till now; and, without the Spirit of the living God to guide them, they will not be able to accomplish anything to their credit towards building up his kingdom. They must realize that success in preaching the Gospel springs not from the wisdom of this world. They must so live as to enjoy the power of God." (In *Journal of Discourses* 8:70–71.)

Preach the Gospel of Jesus Christ

What is the gospel of Jesus Christ? It is the good news, the glad tidings, and all else that causes men and women to repent and "come unto the God of Abraham, and the God of Isaac, and the God of Jacob, and be saved" (1 Nephi 6:4).

The gospel of Jesus Christ embodies truths, covenants, ordinances, and practices that place believers on the path that leads to eternal life. This path begins with steps of repentance, continues with an invitation to be baptized and receive the Holy Ghost, and proceeds with the plea to keep all of the commandments of God and endure to the end. Therefore, it is understandable why the doctrine of the Savior is referred to as the "right way" of living (see 2 Nephi 25:28–29).

Paul the Apostle declared: "I am not ashamed of the gospel of Christ: for it is the power of God unto salvation to every one that believeth" (Romans 1:16). He also said to the Galatians: "There be some that trouble you, and would pervert the gospel of Christ. But though we, or an angel from heaven, preach any other gospel . . . , let him be accursed." (Galatians 1:7–8.)

There is only one true gospel, just as there is only one true and living God. Those who dispute this fact would make God a God of confusion instead of a God of order who can be trusted and relied upon.

How very privileged are the men and women who accept mission calls and go forth preaching, "baptizing with water, saying: Repent ye, repent ye, for the kingdom of heaven is at hand" (D&C 42:7). No greater honor or privilege can be extended to a person than to represent the Lord and serve as a savior of men.

Go About Their Labors "Two by Two"

Anyone who knows the concept of synergism appreciates the wisdom of sending missionaries into the world two by two.

In another place I have written:

> Synergism, it is said, is an old Christian doctrine. It purports that the grace of God combined with the good works of mortals results in full salvation.
>
> In our time, synergism is defined as "the simultaneous action of separate agencies which, together, have greater total effect than the sum of their individual effects" (*Webster's New World Dictionary,* p. 1444).
>
> This principle may be illustrated as follows:
>
> A 2 x 4 eight feet long, standing on end, can bear a weight of 615 pounds. If a second 2 x 4 eight feet long is nailed to the first, together they can bear not 1,230 pounds (double 615 pounds) but rather 2,400 pounds.
>
> . . . Two are not simply twice as strong as one. Two are four times as strong as one [when they are united in the Lord's work]! This is synergism. (Carlos E. Asay, *In the Lord's Service* [Salt Lake City: Deseret Book Co., 1990], pp. 90–91.)

Reasons for serving with others are many and quite apparent. They include the following:

- *The need for two or more witnesses.* The Lord has declared more than once, "In the mouth of two or three witnesses shall every word be established" (2 Corinthians 13:1; see also Deuteronomy 17:6; Matthew 18:16; Ether 5:4; D&C 6:28, 128:3). People serving together teach and bear witness of the work they share. Each testifies of what the other says. Moreover, each witnesses in behalf of the other, refuting the words of false accusers or others who would defile the truth.
- *Support in teaching.* Alma and Amulek constituted a powerful companionship. According to the account in the Book of Mormon, Alma "began to speak . . . and to establish the words of Amulek, and to explain things beyond, or to unfold the scriptures beyond that which Amulek had done" (Alma 12:1). Two minds are, generally speaking, better than one. When both are concentrated upon the same task or purpose, mutual support may be enjoyed.
- *Protection.* The preacher said: "Two are better than one; because they have a good reward for their labour. For if they fall, the one will lift up his fellow: but woe to him that is alone when he falleth; for he hath not another to help him up. . . . And if one prevail against him, two shall withstand him." (Ecclesiastes 4:9–10, 12.)
- *Strengthen one another.* There are many scriptures that explain the need to strengthen those with whom we serve. I shall cite four:
  —"The Lord said, Simon, Simon, behold, Satan hath desired to have you, that he may sift you as wheat: but I have prayed for thee, that thy faith fail not: and when thou art converted, strengthen thy brethren" (Luke 22:31–32).
  —"If any man among you be strong in the Spirit, let him take with him him that is weak, that he may be edified in all meekness, that he may become strong also" (D&C 84:106).
  —"We then that are strong [experienced] ought to bear the infirmities of the weak [inexperienced], and not to

please ourselves. Let every one of us please his [missionary companion] for his good to edification." (Romans 15:1–2.)

—"Strengthen your brethren in all your conversation, in all your prayers, in all your exhortations, and in all your doings" (D&C 108:7).

- *Counsel.* One of the greatest benefits of serving with others relates to counsel. Those older or more experienced share what they have learned; those younger or less experienced provide fresh insights and new enthusiasm. All have something valuable to contribute.

  Alma counseled one of his sons: "I command you to take it upon you to counsel with your elder brothers in your undertakings; for behold, thou art in thy youth, and ye stand in need to be nourished by your brothers. And give heed to their counsel." (Alma 39:10; see also 1 Peter 5:5.)

These are only a few of the benefits of serving with others. More reasons could be listed. Please understand that synergistic powers are unleashed as servants of the Lord witness, support, protect, strengthen, and counsel one another (see Asay, *In the Lord's Service,* pp. 92–93).

Teach and Testify in the Name of the Lord

Missionaries are representatives of the true and living God, and all that they do and say must be done in his holy name. Many prophets have reminded us that there is "no other name given nor any other way nor means whereby salvation can come unto the children of men, only in and through the name of Christ, the Lord Omnipotent" (Mosiah 3:17). Hence, missionaries are expected to labor diligently in persuading others "to believe in Christ, and to be reconciled to God; for we know that it is by grace that we are saved, after all we can do" (2 Nephi 25:23).

When we pray, we address God the Father, he whom we lovingly refer to as our Heavenly Father. Each prayer is closed in the name of Jesus Christ, he who is the Only Begotten Son of God and whom we adore as the Savior of mankind. We belong to the Church or household of God that bears the name of him who is the "chief corner stone" of the organization (Ephesians 2:20). Moreover, legal administrators in the Church, including missionaries, officiate and perform all ordinances in the name of Christ.

It would be an inconsistency of serious proportions if missionaries did not teach and testify in the name of the Lord. Missionaries have taken upon themselves his holy name, and they have agreed to stand as his witnesses "at all times and in all things, and in all places" (Mosiah 18:9).

Lift Up Their Voices "as with the Voice of a Trump" (D&C 29:4)

A rebellious young man by the name of Alma was rebuked by an angel who spoke with "a voice of thunder, which caused the earth to shake" (Mosiah 27:11). Later on, after Alma had repented and cleaned up his life, he wished that he were an angel and that he could speak "with the trump of God, with a voice to shake the earth, and cry repentance unto every people!" (Alma 29:1.) That same wish or desire should be in the heart of every missionary.

There was an occasion when elders of the Church were reluctant to open their mouths and lift up their voices. The Lord chastised them by saying, "But with some I am not well pleased, for they will not open their mouths, but they hide the talent which I have given unto them, because of the fear of man" (D&C 60:2).

Sometimes missionaries are ridiculed, rejected, and scoffed at by those who are hard of heart and blind of mind. Perhaps part of such rejection is related to unpreparedness or a weakness of testimony. However, those who study, prepare, live righteously, and open their mouths are promised that they shall be filled and blessed with success. (See D&C 33:2, 8–10.)

Only the faithless hide their talents and go about their proselyting work apologetically. But those with faith and an understanding of what the gospel can do to liberate people from the abyss of sin and elevate them into a condition of exquisite joy willfully lift up their voices as with the sound of a trump.

Declare God's Word "like unto Angels" (D&C 42:6)

Speaking of angels, Mormon taught: "The office of their ministry is to call men unto repentance, and to fulfil and to do the work of the covenants of the Father, which he hath made unto the children of men, to prepare the way among the children of men, by declaring the word of Christ unto the chosen vessels of the Lord, that they may bear testimony of him" (Moroni 7:31).

Almost the same could be said about the office and calling of full-time missionaries. They too are commissioned to call men to repentance, to do the will of the Father, and to declare the word of Christ to the people of the world. They too receive an unction or anointing from the Holy One to teach, testify, and search out the chosen vessels of the Lord (see 1 John 2:20, 27).

In the course of their ministries, many missionaries are treated by people "as though they were angels sent from God to save them from everlasting destruction" (Alma 27:4). Some missionaries become so sanctified through their service that their faces "shine exceedingly, even as the faces of angels" (Helaman 5:36). More than a few become imbued with the Spirit and wish that they were angels so that they could speak with "a voice to shake the earth, and cry repentance unto every people!" (Alma 29:1.) Little wonder that God extends missionaries the promise: "I will go before your face. I will be on your right hand and on your left, and my Spirit shall be in your hearts, and mine angels round about you, to bear you up." (D&C 84:88.)

Much more could be said about the six-fold angelic commission given to full-time missionaries. The call is clear, and the expectations are explicit. I would add only these words of the Prophet Joseph Smith given at the dedication of the Kirtland Temple: "And we ask thee, Holy Father, that thy servants may go forth from this house armed with thy power, and that thy name may be upon them, and thy glory be round about them, and thine angels have charge over them" (D&C 109:22).

Instruments of Righteousness

As a small boy in grammar school, I had a teacher who made King Arthur and the Knights of the Round Table come alive for me. She caused me to become so obsessed with stories of knights that I played and dreamed that I was one.

One evening I dreamed that I was a white knight on a white horse riding over the greens of England. Suddenly, without warning, a knight dressed in black armor and mounted on a black horse appeared at the edge of the forest. We measured each other carefully, lowered our lances, and charged at full gallop. The lances struck target, and both of us were knocked off our steeds.

I scrambled to my feet, knowing that we would draw our swords and that hand-to-hand combat was imminent. Fear gripped my heart as I saw my opponent rushing toward me flashing a long, gleaming sword. Instinctively I reached to my side and drew forth from the scabbard my weapon. That is when the dream turned into a nightmare! In my hand was a tiny dagger—not a long, gleaming sword. I woke up in a cold sweat, screaming for help.

Many times since that nightmarish experience, I have wondered about the serviceability of the Saints. When God calls us to serve, are we positioned in the scabbard and ready to be drawn? When the Lord draws us forth as his instrument in combating evil forces, what does he have in his hand—a long, gleaming sword or a dinky dagger?

Shared Opportunities

At one time I wondered why God did not take matters into his own hands and guarantee the salvation of all people. I knew that God was omnipotent and could, if he so willed, thunder his word over the earth and blaze his message across the skies with such convincing power that everyone would join the Church. I also knew he could build all the temples needed, perform all the family history research required, and do all else—single-handedly, letter-perfect, and without any wasted motion. Yes, I knew that God could do it all by simple command, without the help or intrusion of weak mortals.

As my understanding of the gospel of Jesus Christ expanded, I saw the folly of a one-man show. I realized that if Heavenly Father took matters into his own hands and performed all the missionary, temple, and other Church services, he would: (1) offend our agency in a manner similar to what Lucifer proposed before the world was formed (see Moses 4:1–3), and (2) deprive us of sanctifying experiences, just as impatient, perfectionist parents deprive their children of growth when they push the children aside and do all the work themselves. These and other gospel insights led me to the conclusion that an all-wise and loving Father involves his children in his work so they may grow, learn, and become like him.

Opposite Forces

From the very beginning, our Heavenly Father has worked through his children in fulfilling his holy purposes. It was through his Only Begotten Son that the Atonement was wrought. Another son, Adam, became the father of the whole human family. Moses led the children of Israel out of bondage. A modern Joseph became the prophet of the Restoration. All of these leaders served as agents or instruments in the hands of God in helping to fulfill his avowed purpose of bringing "to pass the immortality and eternal life of man" (Moses 1:39). Each was sanctified and assumed attributes of the Father in the process.

Other children of God listened to another voice, a dissident voice, and made themselves instruments of the outcast Satan. This was done in fulfillment of Lucifer's pledge "to deceive and to blind men, and to lead them captive at his will" (Moses 4:4), for he had warned that he would fight his battles and extend his rule through those who loved darkness more than light.

Satan used the hands of Cain in committing murder (see Moses 5:16–35); he used Korihor as his voice in preaching anti-Christian doctrine (see Alma 30:6–21); and he abused Sherem's learned nature and perfect knowledge of language by having him sow seeds of doubt among the Nephites (see Jacob 7:1–20). In each of these instances, Cain, Korihor, or Sherem yielded himself to Satan and became an instrument of unrighteousness. Each was abandoned in the end by his tempter and allowed to go down in bitter defeat (see Alma 30:60).

Yield Yourselves to God

The Apostle Paul understood clearly the life-and-death struggle for the souls of men. He was aware of the enlistment programs of both sides—the Savior and his Saints, and Lucifer and his legions. Therefore he issued this warning to the Romans: "Neither yield ye your members as instruments of unrighteousness unto sin: but yield yourselves unto God, as those that are alive from the dead, and your members as instruments of righteousness unto God" (Romans 6:13). He added, "Know ye not, that to whom ye yield yourselves servants to obey, his servants ye are to whom ye obey; whether of sin unto death, or of obedience unto righteousness?" (Romans 6:16.)

To yield is to give or submit oneself. So the first issue is, are you positioned in the scabbard of righteousness and ready to be drawn by the hand of God? Alma and the sons of Mosiah, through disobedience, allowed themselves to slip into the wrong sheath. An evil hand drew them forth and caused them to become an impediment to the church of God. This period of subjection to Satan was later referred to by Alma as the "gall of bitterness," "bonds of iniquity," and "darkest abyss" (Mosiah 27:29).

After a miraculous conversion, Alma and his friends changed scabbards. They confessed their sins, tried to repair the injuries they had made, and published peace. According to the record, "They were instruments in the hands of God in bringing many to the knowledge of the truth, yea, to the knowledge of their Redeemer" (Mosiah 27:36).

The slide into Satan's scabbard begins with little and seemingly harmless transgressions. It may start with a cigarette, a suggestive thought, an off-color story, one alcoholic drink, a so-called white lie, or even one X-rated movie. Gradually, however, the sins mount in number and seriousness until one finds himself Satan's ward. Each wrongdoing molds the transgressor's hilt to fit the hand of Lucifer.

In contrast, properly directed faith, repentance, and good works guide one into the scabbard strapped to the side of Deity. The person who cultivates a love for the scriptures, attends church, becomes involved in service projects, prays daily and honestly, and honors loving parents is positioning himself or herself for righteous service. A state of useful readiness is achieved virtue by virtue as the hilt of the instrument and the hand of God become molded as one.

Gleaming Swords or Dinky Daggers?

Now, the second issue: When the Lord draws you forth to wage his battles, does he have in his hand a long, gleaming sword? If I were a knight and I was preparing for combat, I would select carefully the tools of my trade. At the top of my list of tools would be a strong, sharp, and gleaming sword. I would want a sword that was perfectly balanced and honed to a fine cutting edge. It would be of the finest steel and fitted so perfectly to my hand that it felt like an extension of my arm. I would not want to be hindered by a small, useless weapon that I could have little confidence in. A long, gleaming sword, however, would reflect light and power; it would stir confidence in the heart of its user and strike fear into the heart of its intended target.

Strong, Sharp, and Clean

To observers in Jerusalem of a former day, Peter may have appeared to be a small, useless weapon as he denied Christ thrice near the high priest's palace (see Matthew 26:69–75). But when the converted Peter stood before the Jews on the day of Pentecost, he testified with the conviction and power of a gleaming sword, placing himself in the hands of God and winning the souls of three thousand people (see Acts 2).

The mettle of the man Peter did not come automatically and without effort. Peter was subjected to trials and temptations and all else commonly referred to as the refiner's fire. The heat of opposition did not consume him; it served only to burn out the impurities and weaknesses and leave refined and pure metal. Peter emerged from the furnace of affliction as a polished, strong sword of righteousness. His iron strength of character carried him through to the end of his mission.

After the day of Pentecost, Peter was a man with a cutting edge. He exhibited a sharpness of mind that enabled him to bear witness of the risen Christ. It is recorded that on one occasion his words "cut to the heart" (Acts 5:33) those who sought to slay him. Undoubtedly such sharpness of mind was the result of much study, fasting, and prayer.

We are taught that miracles are performed and revelation received through clean vessels of the Lord (see 3 Nephi 8:1). Peter's cleanliness of soul gained him deliverance from prison at the hands of angels. It provided him power to heal the sick and raise Dorcas from death (see Acts 9:36–42). And his purity made it possible for him to see a vision that led to the extension of the gospel to the Gentiles.

The saving virtue of a sword is related to its strength, sharpness, and cleanliness and to the hand that guides it. Is it not the same with people? (See Asay, *In the Lord's Service*, pp. 58–64.)

Schoolboys or Missionaries?

A number of years ago, two missionaries walked along a street in a large city in Europe. It was a lovely morning, and their enthusiasm for life was reflected in their brisk walk and jovial moods. When one missionary was least expecting it, the other kicked his companion's heel and sent him stumbling forward. Both laughed boisterously over the little trick and merrily went on their way. Later, when the kicking elder had relaxed his guard, the companion returned the favor with added vigor that almost caused a serious fall on the pavement. Once again, however, they laughed and continued down the sidewalk.

The next day they tracted along that same street. At one door, a lady appeared and extended a warm greeting. Quickly the senior companion announced, "We are representatives of the Lord Jesus Christ. We have a—" At that point, the woman interrupted the elder by saying: "No, you can't be representatives of the Lord. Representatives of the Lord would not walk down the street laughing and joking like two little schoolboys, as you did yesterday."

In this instance, the missionaries did not match the message they were bearing. Their actions betrayed their purpose and mocked the one they represented.

Christlike Preparation and Growth

If a missionary truly desires to become an instrument of righteousness—even a sharp, gleaming sword—in the hands of God, there are certain honing actions that must be taken. To begin with, he must increase "in wisdom and stature, and in favour with God and man" (Luke 2:52). Don't forget, the Savior "received not of the fulness at the first, but received grace for grace" (D&C 93:12), and so must all who seek to become his worthy servants.

An *increase in wisdom* occurs as one "seek[s] learning, even by study and also by faith" (D&C 88:118). I know of a young man who entered the mission field with little or no grounding in the gospel. Consequently he embarrassed himself and the Lord during his first teaching appointment. He was so mortified by the experience that he pledged to God that he would search the scriptures, seek the Spirit, and thirst after the proper knowledge, if only the Lord would forgive him and bless him. In just a few short months he became a gospel scholar and one of the most effective teachers in his mission.

An increase in wisdom refers to an enlightenment of understanding and an expansion of the mind as pertaining to the teachings of the Lord (see Alma 32:28, 34). Such enlightenment and expansion occurs as one searches the scriptures, ponders the written and spoken words of prophets, and receives personal insights and revelation. It occurs with those who thirst after righteousness and drink freely of living waters (see John 4:1–14).

An *increase in stature* suggests physical growth and well-being. Many young people mature and put on inches and pounds while serving as full-time missionaries. They begin their ministries as young and raw individuals, but they arise from their inexperience and become men and women of Christ. Sooner or later they learn that fitness to serve is not a gift, freely endowed to all persons. Real and complete fitness is attained through proper diet, regular exercise, adequate rest, clean living, and good medical care.

Life, even missionary life, can become a burden to those who neglect their physical machines. It is virtually impossible for a missionary to be effective and happy when plagued with fatigue or illness. Worse still, when one is idled by sickness, the companion is also restricted in his or her activities. As William Osler observed, "The clean tongue, the clear head, and the bright eye are birthrights of each [missionary] day" (*A Way of Life* [New York: Harper and Brothers, 1937], p. 25).

Elder John A. Widtsoe is reported to have said: "There should be no pride in ill health. The person who keeps his body in good condition lengthens out his life in years, and, because he can do his work more effectively, increases the sum total of his service and enjoyments on earth." Of course, there are missionaries who become ill through no fault of their own. The Lord tells us that no one is to run faster than his or her strength (see Mosiah 4:27).

An *increase in favor with God* implies spiritual growth by yielding to "the enticings of the Holy Spirit" and putting off "the natural man" (Mosiah 3:19). A missionary begins the process by controlling his thoughts and garnishing them with virtue. He continues by measuring his words carefully and speaking only the truth. He distances himself from fleshly desires and influences by studying, praying, and working diligently. Gradually, day by day, he becomes more and more like the sons of Mosiah. Of them it was said: "They had waxed strong in the knowledge of the truth; for they were men of a sound understanding and they had searched the scriptures diligently, that they might know the word of God. But this is not all; they had given themselves to much prayer, and fasting; therefore they had the spirit of prophecy, and the spirit of revelation, and when they taught, they taught with power and authority of God." (Alma 17:2–3.)

A missionary's transformation does not take place automatically without some pain and persistent effort. I like the words of a country sheepherder who, despite the rocky beginning of his mission, eventually gained favor with God. In answer to the question, How did you do it? he replied, "I just realized one day how raw I was, how poorly equipped to do the Lord's work. So I buckled down and changed my ways and my outlook, and studied hard, and began to do not what I wanted to do, but what the Lord asked me to do. I still have far to go. But I've started." (Quoted in Robert O'Brien, *Marriott: The J. Willard Marriott Story* [Salt Lake City: Deseret Book Co., 1977], p. 74.)

An increase in favor with man affirms the need for missionaries to develop all of the social graces consistent with their divine callings. President Joseph F. Smith taught, "The characteristics of a good missionary are: A man who has sociability—whose friendship is permanent and sparkling—who can ingratiate himself into the confidence and favor of men who are in darkness" (*Gospel Doctrine* [Salt Lake City: Deseret Book Co., 1919], p. 356).

Hyrum M. Smith and Janne M. Sjodahl add: "A successful missionary has the faculty of making friends. He takes an interest in all that interests his fellowmen, and brings to the society in which he moves the sweet influence of the gospel, even when he does not say a word on the subject of religion. Hermits are useless as missionaries." (*Doctrine and Covenants Commentary*, rev. ed. [Salt Lake City: Deseret Book Co., 1951], p. 728 n. 3.)

I would add only the caution given by Brigham Young: "If you go on a mission to preach the Gospel with lightness and frivolity in your hearts, looking for this and that, and to learn what is in the world, and not having your minds riveted . . . on the cross of Christ, you will go and return in vain" (*Discourses of Brigham Young*, sel. John A. Widtsoe [Salt Lake City: Deseret Book Co., 1978], p. 325).

Christlike preparation and growth may be capsulized in the simple but meaningful entreaty, "Be strong in the Lord, and in the power of his might. Put on the whole armour of God." (Ephesians 6:10–11.) All soldiers of the Spirit or good soldiers of Jesus Christ will—

—Have their "*loins girt* about with truth."
—Put on "the *breastplate* of righteousness."
—Shod their *feet* "with the preparation of the gospel of peace."
—Take in hand "the *shield* of faith."
—Don "the *helmet* of salvation."
—Wield "the *sword* of the Spirit, which is the word of God."
—And pray always for needed support.
(See Ephesians 6:14–18; see also D&C 27:15–18.)

Serve with the Whole Soul

I don't suppose that any missionary ever feels fully and adequately prepared to represent Deity. If one does, one may be dangerously close to losing one's humility and feeling of dependency upon the Lord. If one runs a little scared in one's calling, recognizing the continuing need to improve one's performance and rely upon the Lord, one will never forget that it is really God who works the miracles and gives the increase.

No amount of preparation and success ever supersedes the following command given to those who serve in God's kingdom, especially full-time missionaries: "Therefore, O ye that embark in the service of God, see that ye serve him with all your heart, might, mind and strength, that ye may stand blameless before God at the last day" (D&C 4:2).

I emphasize those four powerful words: heart, might, mind, and strength. Authors Smith and Sjodahl explain: "'Heart' stands for 'emotions', 'sentiment'. 'Might' . . . stands for 'soul' . . . and means the spiritual faculties. 'Mind' refers to the intellect, and 'strength' to the physical attributes. This commandment enjoins on us to love our heavenly Father so that our entire beings—our emotions, our spiritual faculties, and mental and physical activities are all devoted to Him and His service." (*Doctrine and Covenants Commentary*, p. 350.)

Missionary service is really a matter of love and faith. Those who love the Lord and have faith in him and his stated purposes will "come unto him, and offer [their] whole souls as an offering unto him" (Omni 1:26). Those whose love and faith is weak are prone to withhold their services and lose the blessings.

A Proselyting Model

A number of scriptural references provide proper directions for missionaries. For instance, Ammon won the hearts of a people through *service* (see Alma 17:23–30); Peter and John spoke "the word of God *with boldness*" (Acts 4:31; emphasis added); Aaron *opened the scriptures* to his listeners and discussed the plan of salvation and the coming of Christ (see Alma 21:9); the sons of Mosiah gained power *through fasting and prayer* (see Alma 17:3); Apollos was "*an eloquent man, and mighty in the scriptures*" (Acts 18:24; emphasis added); and Paul *tailored his remarks* to catch the attention of people worshipping an "unknown God" (see Acts 17:22–31). These and many more references give us valuable insights concerning the behavior of effective missionaries.

However, I know of only one concise listing of missionary virtues in holy writ that constitutes a comprehensive model worthy of close inspection by all full-time proselyters. This listing is found in the first epistle of Paul to the Thessalonians, chapter 2, verses 1–13. I will lead you through Paul's record verse by verse and make brief comments. In the end, a proselyting model emerges for true ministers who desire to preach in a godly manner—a manner that never becomes timeworn, out-of-date, or inappropriate.

Verse 1: "For yourselves, brethren, know our entrance in unto you, that it was not in vain."

I have no idea how many converts Paul won among the Thessalonians. It is presumed that his harvest of souls was significant because the group is referred to collectively as "the church" (1 Thessalonians 1:1). Moreover, the very fact that Paul addressed at least two letters to these people suggests a community of Saints worthy of receiving bolstering correspondence from their concerned leader. So, whatever the number of converts, Paul's work was not in vain—it was a success!

All missionaries should be success-oriented, as was Paul. They should serve with resolve and determination, believing that their honest efforts will not be in vain. Feelings of doubt, defeat, and despair are satanic and must be dispelled. True ministers mirror the optimism and courage of these lines: "Go forward and not backward. Courage, brethren; and on, on to the victory!" (D&C 128:22.)

Even if Paul's work in Thessalonica had resulted only in strengthening his personal conversion and in the writing of two inspired epistles, it would not have been wasted. Missionary success cannot and must not be measured only by the number of converts gained. There are other standards involved, such as testimony and goodness, that cannot be counted or reduced to simple numbers and figures.

Poor performance, however, must not be rationalized by referring to the unmeasurable aspects of missionary service. Each missionary is accountable for his or her efforts, and each should be open to an inspection of his or her records.

Verse 2: "But even after that we had suffered before, and were shamefully entreated, as ye know, at Philippi, we were bold in our God to speak unto you the gospel of God with much contention [confidence]."

Men and women of weak faith or conviction wilt under the heat of opposition. Shameful entreatment can cause quick retreat. Rejection can cause submissiveness and subjection.

But Paul was not to be denied. He was a fearless witness of Christ in many life-threatening circumstances. He was bold in his God because he was strong in his faith and confident in his message.

Modern missionaries must also possess this virtue. It can be said that faith causes a man to stand, authority prompts him to stand tall, and testimony enables him to stand tall and firm. Mormon wrote: "Behold, I speak with boldness, having authority from God; and I fear not what man can do; for perfect love casteth out all fear" (Moroni 8:16).

Said Alma to his son Shiblon, "Use boldness, but not overbearance" (Alma 38:12). I believe that Alma was advocating a type of confidence relating to a commission received of God and a confidence relating to a righteous life. If a missionary or member really believes that he or she is an agent of the Lord and engaged in the Lord's business, that person's confidence and boldness will wax strong, providing he or she is doing things according to the will of the Lord (see D&C 64:29; Proverbs 28:1).

Verse 3: "For our exhortation was not of deceit, nor of uncleanness, nor in guile."

The Apostle Paul might well have said: "We taught you the pure unadulterated truth from the scriptures, and we did it in an honest, forthright manner." There was no high-powered salesmanship in Paul's approach; there was no gimmickry involved or attempts to delude his listeners. Paul knew the sacredness of his message and the holiness of his calling, and he kept himself free of tactics and strategies that would mock or demean his important mission.

The same must be said of today's missionaries and members. It is wrong to trifle with the souls of men and women by engaging in cursing conversations or speaking half-truths. Is it possible that the Lord had this in mind when he taught: "Not that which goeth into the mouth defileth a man; but that which cometh out of the mouth, this defileth a man" (Matthew 15:11).

Verse 4: "But as we were allowed of God to be put in trust with the gospel, even so we speak; not as pleasing men, but God, which trieth our hearts" (emphasis added).

One marvels, like Paul, at the trust that God places in his children. He makes them custodians of his saving truths; he places in their hands the salvation of precious souls; and he relies upon them to build his church and kingdom upon the earth. What greater things could he possibly put in their trust?

If a missionary's or member's trust came from men, that would be one thing. But since the trust is of the Lord, it should be regarded soberly and seriously. It should try one's heart to the extent that it provokes a godly manner of living and preaching. It should also cause one to heed this counsel: "Wherefore, be not weary in well-doing, for ye are laying the foundation of a great work. And out of small things proceedeth that which is great. Before, the Lord requireth the heart and a willing mind; and the willing and obedient shall eat the good of the land of Zion in these last days." (D&C 64:33–34.)

Verse 5: "For neither at any time used we flattering words, as ye know, nor a cloke of covetousness; God is witness."

Flattery is defined as insincere and excessive praise. It is a device used by the evil one to lull people into a false sense of security and a procrastination of repentance. Sherem, an anti-Christ, was learned and had a perfect knowledge of the language of the people; "wherefore," it is written, "he could use much flattery, and much power of speech, according to the power of the devil" (Jacob 7:4).

Paul and other true ministers do not hide behind a "cloke of covetousness" or resort to flattery to accomplish their purposes. They know that sin must be identified and forsaken, else there would be no progress upward. They know that friendships based upon ear-tickling exchanges are shallow and short-lived. They also know that calls to repentance and commitments to live the commandments, voiced in a spirit of sincere love and concern, will weld friendships between missionaries and contacts rather than destroy them.

Verse 6: "Nor of men sought we glory, neither of you, nor yet of others, when we might have been burdensome, as the apostles of Christ."

The power of a person seems to be directly related to his motive. If he serves with an eye over his shoulder expecting the praise and adulation of others, his powers are limited to his own resources. If, however, his heart is right and he ascribes the honor and glory to the Lord with a singleness of mind, he draws powers from above.

Verse 7: "But we were gentle among you, even as a nurse cherisheth her children."

Years ago I was stricken with a serious illness and not expected to live. Family members were summoned, and they paraded by my bedside to say good-bye. I was unconscious most of the time and racked with fever and pain. I can recall seeing only one or two persons. However, there was a nurse whom I shall never forget and in whose debt I shall always be. During the crisis hours, she sat at my side gently rubbing my arms to aid the circulation and whispering softly in my ear over and over again: "You must not die! You will live!"

In many respects, missionaries are like nurses. They assist the Great Physician in the healing arts of the gospel. They seek to reduce the number of spiritual deaths. Such is done by helping people recognize spiritual illnesses and by applying the cures of faith, repentance, baptism, and other gospel principles.

True ministers work their miracles "by persuasion, by long-suffering, by gentleness and meekness, and by love unfeigned; by kindness, and pure knowledge, which shall greatly enlarge the soul without hypocrisy, and without guile" (D&C 121:41–42). Like my nurse, they minister selflessly and encourage people to overcome sin and the other enemies of the soul.

Verse 8: "So being affectionately desirous of you, we were willing to have imparted unto you, not the gospel of God only, but also our own souls, because ye were dear unto us."

This is a tender statement. In it, Paul expresses a love for the Saints in Thessalonica that is deep and abiding. His love apparently reached the point that he loved the people as much or more than himself. Little wonder they responded so well to his instructions!

Paul's words bring to mind something the Savior taught: "He that findeth his life shall lose it: and he that loseth his life for my sake shall find it" (Matthew 10:39). Moreover, "Greater love hath no man than this, that a man lay down his life for his friends" (John 15:13).

It is a good and noble thing to share one's testimony with another. Yet that gift, as precious as it is, has limited value unless it is given with charity—"the pure love of Christ" (Moroni 7:47). One cannot preach or minister in a godly manner until this type of love for people is cultivated. And such love is cultivated by serving others, looking for the best in others, withholding judgment of others, and viewing others in terms of what they may become rather than who they are.

I would ask, who loves children most? The answer is mother. Why? Because she serves her children and gives them her all. Similarly, through service missionaries learn to love people regardless of race, color, creed, and standard of living.

Verse 9: "For ye remember, brethren, our labour and travail: for labouring night and day, because we would not be charge-

able unto any of you, we preached unto you the gospel of God" (emphasis added).

I emphasize the words *labor* and *travail*. Both are synonymous for work; however, *travail* suggests very hard work. Apparently Paul made such a full investment of himself in preaching to the Thessalonians that he concluded his efforts with a clear conscience.

If he does his best and serves in the Lord's appointed way, a missionary can "stand blameless before God at the last day" (D&C 4:2), or declare that he is not chargeable to the people he serves. Otherwise, he completes his work with a troublesome conscience and wishes that he had been more faithful. (See Ezekiel 3:17–21; Jacob 1:19, 2:2; Mosiah 2:27.)

Verse 10: "Ye are witnesses, and God also, how holily and justly and unblameably we behaved ourselves among you that believe."

Righteous or model behavior is the godly attribute highlighted by Paul in this verse. Obviously, he had lived as he taught Timothy: "Be thou an example of the believers, in word, in conversation, in charity, in spirit, in faith, in purity" (1 Timothy 4:12).

Paul did not allow his actions to mock his words, nor should any other representative of the Lord.

Much of our communication is nonverbal. Who we are and what we do count for more than what we say. Therefore, missionaries must act well their parts and avoid all forms of hypocrisy.

While presiding over a mission, I received an anonymous telephone call from a nonmember. The woman said: "I have watched your missionaries come and go in my neighborhood for years, and I have grown to appreciate them for their cleanliness and circumspect behavior. But," she added, "the two who are currently laboring in this part of the city are not living as they should." I promptly investigated the matter and, to my chagrin, verified the woman's report. In this isolated case, two negligent missionaries had forgotten their holy callings and were chargeable to both God and the people who had been offended by their actions. As happened with Corianton of old, the wayward behavior or conduct of the missionaries had caused investigators to reject the truth (see Alma 39:10–12).

Men and women of Christ are what is needed in missionary service—men and women who are "a light unto the world" (D&C 103:9).

Verse 11: "As ye know how we exhorted and comforted and charged every one of you, as a father doth his children."

This verse refers to the teaching approach used by Paul and his coworkers and the manner in which the approach was used. In modern language we would say: They taught (exhorted), resolved concerns (comforted), and committed (charged) their listeners. And, we would add, their actions were an outgrowth of their profound love for the people.

We can surmise from the scripture that the missionaries in the meridian of time understood what we have learned in the fulness of times, namely: "Faith, if it hath not works, is dead" (James 2:17); both gospel principles and saving ordinances are necessary; spiritual rebirth requires understanding and commitment; and the grace of God and the good works of man work synergistically toward salvation. Otherwise Paul and his associates would not have attempted to resolve the concerns of the people or challenge them to accept a higher form of living.

It is imperative that modern missionaries teach and testify and invite contacts to make needed changes in their lives. At the same time, they must remember that there is no place for force or coercion in missionary work. It must always be a labor of love, wherein those who exhort and charge exercise a parental type of loving concern and those who accept do so much like a trusting child.

Verse 12: "That ye would walk worthy of God, who hath called you unto his kingdom and glory."

In my mind, this verse has an implicit and an implied meaning. The implicit meaning is that Paul wanted his converts to remain true to the faith. He did not want them to fall away or out of the Church. He wanted the fruits of his labors to remain. He knew that their retention depended upon their continuing resolve to walk worthy of the Spirit (see John 15:16).

Missionaries or members must be interested in more than baptisms. They must be intent upon obtaining *convert* baptisms. They must understand that "conversion is not a point but a line, not the beginning of a Christian life but the whole of it." Their duty is to place themselves on that line, walk progressively forward, and invite others to do the same. Full-time missionaries and member-missionaries understand that they enjoy their present blessings through the grace of God and full obedience to the laws and ordinances of the gospel; therefore, they reach out with love to help others walk the path marked by the Savior. (See *Encyclopedia of Religion and Ethics*, ed. James Hastings, 12 vols. [New York: Charles Scribner's Sons, 1922], 12:161.)

The implied meaning of Paul's words in verse 12 is that missionaries must walk worthy of God—worthy of the Holy Spirit—in order to be effective in their callings. I say this because conversion is really a spiritual transfusion involving the missionary, the investigator, and the Holy Spirit. The missionary teaches under the influence of the Spirit; the Spirit bears witness of the spoken truth; and the investigator responds to the influence of the Spirit by submitting to baptism. It can be said that the missionary sparks a courtship between his or her listener and the Spirit, a courtship that will hopefully become a lifetime companionship.

The Lord promised Enoch: "Behold my Spirit is upon you, wherefore all thy words will I justify; and the mountains shall flee before you, and the rivers shall turn from their course; and thou shalt abide in me, and I in you; therefore walk with me" (Moses 6:34).

Verse 13: "For this cause also thank we God without ceasing, because, when ye received the word of God which ye heard of us, ye received it not as the word of men, but as it is in truth, the word of God, which effectually worketh also in you that believe" *(emphasis added).*

I emphasize the words "ye received . . . as the . . . word of God, which effectually worketh also in you that believe," for they suggest that conversion occurred and a retention of converts took place.

In too many instances, potential converts receive the missionaries and become attached to them rather than to the message. Consequently, when the missionary is transferred or released, the prospective member falls away because he or she is not rooted in the truth. Missionaries must therefore do all that is essential to make the word of God work effectually in the lives of those with whom they labor; otherwise new members will not have "root in themselves" and will "endure but for a time" (Mark 4:17; see also John 15:16).

The missionaries' message of truth will be effective in the lives of others as the hands of converts are placed upon the iron rod (1 Nephi 11:25) and as their hands are clasped by fellow citizens in "the household of God" (see Ephesians 2:19–22, 4:11–16).

Elder Bruce R. McConkie provides this summary of Paul's proselyting model: "The manner in which the Lord's ministers carry their message to the world is one of the great identifying characteristics of the truth. Paul here recites the valiance and devotion, the uprightness and gentleness, the fairness and holiness that attended his missionary efforts and those of his companions. He and they manifest the same spirit and course which the Lord set for his latter-day ministers in these words: 'No one can assist in this work except he shall be humble and full of love, having faith, hope, and charity, being temperate in all things, whatsoever shall be entrusted to his care.' (D&C 12:8)." (*Doctrinal New Testament Commentary*, 3 vols. [Salt Lake City: Bookcraft, 1973], 3:45.)

Summary

All who strive to share the gospel should review periodically the model or standard of service outlined by the Apostle Paul. From time to time you should use Paul's listing of attributes as a mirror. Look into it, and allow it to reflect your personal performance. If you feel that you have not measured up completely in one respect or another, have the courage to make the necessary adjustments.

Don't become discouraged or impatient. Habits are changed slowly. Virtues, like principles, are acquired line upon line, little by little, and day by day. Just maintain your resolve and earnest desire for improvement—the rest will take care of itself.

The kind of men we want as bearers of this Gospel message are men who have faith in God; men who have faith in their religion; men who honor their Priesthood; men in whom the people who know them have faith

and in whom God has confidence, and not some poor unfortunate beings who are wanted to leave a place because they cannot live in it; but we want men full of the Holy Ghost and the power of God that they may go forth . . . sowing the seeds of eternal life, and then returning with gladness, bringing their sheaves with them. . . . Men who bear the words of life among the nations, ought to be men of honor, integrity, virtue and purity; and this being the command of God to us, we shall try and carry it out. (John Taylor, in Journal of Discourses 21:375.)

5

METHODS

Use of Every Honorable Means

Know this, that ev'ry soul is free
To choose his life and what he'll be;
For this eternal truth is giv'n:
That God will force no man to heav'n.

He'll call, persuade, direct aright,
And bless with wisdom, love, and light,
In nameless ways be good and kind,
But never force the human mind.
("Know This, That Every Soul Is Free," in Hymns, no. 240.)

The fifth M of missionary service is methods—those honorable means employed in finding, friendshipping, teaching, baptizing, and fellowshipping honest investigators of the truth.

Truth is tainted when forced upon another person, just as food is polluted when served with a dirty spoon. The same applies to the sharing of a testimony. It too loses much of its efficacy when expressed in harsh words or in intimidating tones of voice. Something as valuable as the gospel of Jesus Christ should be packaged and passed with tender, loving care from one friend to another like the pearl of great price that it is.

Successful proselyting methods vary from person to person and from place to place. The service approach works among some people. Door-to-door tracting may or may not be effective. Some do well by using the Book of Mormon to introduce their message. Others like to begin by establishing the fact that we are Christians. The plan of salvation discussion is interesting and captivating to most. However, the wise and successful member or missionary has a variety of methods and approaches, all based upon sound proselyting principles, that he or she tailors to meet the needs of people and ever-changing circumstances.

Basic Actions—Teach, Testify, Exemplify

Reduced to its simplest form, the acceptable methodology of sharing the gospel of Christ is teach, testify, and exemplify. It was said "that Jesus began both to do and teach" (Acts 1:1). Of one ancient prophet, it is written: "For Ezra had prepared his heart *to seek* the law of the Lord, and *to do* it, and *to teach* in Israel statutes and judgments" (Ezra 7:10; emphasis added). Teaching and testifying by precept and example—these actions constitute the core and kernel of the proselyting process.

Teaching is an appeal to the mind; testifying is an appeal to the heart; and exemplifying is an appeal to do what someone else has done. Though each is vital to the process, all three are interrelated and together provide an appeal to the whole soul of man.

A modern revelation reads: "Wherefore, I the Lord ask you this question—unto what were ye ordained? To preach my gospel by the Spirit, even the Comforter which was sent forth to teach the truth. . . . Wherefore, he that preacheth and he that receiveth, understand one another, and both are edified and rejoice together." (D&C 50:13–14, 22.)

Members and missionaries should remember that a listener may take issue with things taught; we do, after all, have minds of our own and differences of opinion. However, that same listener will seldom quarrel with sincere expressions of testimony, for testimony comes from within and cannot be disputed. When teaching and testifying are bolstered by honest efforts to *show* the listener "a more excellent way" (1 Corinthians 12:31), hearts are touched and lives are changed.

Pure Religion

The process of teaching, testifying, and exemplifying becomes more meaningful when related to the practice of pure religion, as depicted below in triangular form:

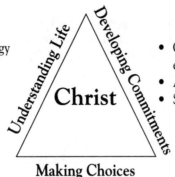

Knowing (Mind)

- Acquiring a theology or set of beliefs
- Cognitive learning
- Mental affirmation

Feeling (Heart)

- Gaining spiritual and emotional experiences
- Affective learning
- Spiritual confirmation

Making Choices

Doing (Hand)

- Engaging in good works or proper actions
- Applied learning
- Conversion of the whole soul (to do and to become)

The Savior

Please note that Christ is the center of the triangle—the center of pure religion. His name is the only name given "whereby salvation can come unto the children of men" (Mosiah 3:17), and he is the one to whom our children must look as the only source for "a remission of their sins" (2 Nephi 25:26). He is the Savior and Redeemer of all mankind, and he is our advocate with the Father. To practice pure religion, we must know Christ, love him, serve him, and worship him in spirit and in truth (see 2 Nephi 25:28–29).

Just as the Savior is the center of pure religion, so also is he the center of the methods or procedures used in declaring his saving truths. Hence, his representatives and advocates must gain a testimony of his life and mission. You must talk of him, rejoice in him, and preach of him with sincerity and conviction. You must know his word and strive to follow in his steps (see 1 Peter 2:21).

King Benjamin asked: "For how knoweth a man the master whom he has not served, and who is a stranger unto him, and is far from the thoughts and intents of his heart?" (Mosiah 5:13.) The answer to this question is obvious. Those who refuse to think of him and serve him will never know him. Those who do center their thoughts, words, and deeds in him will not only know him but become partakers of those precious gifts of immortality and eternal life that he offers all mankind without money or price.

It is, therefore, most important that members and missionaries declare Christ's generation and invite all to become his seed, or heirs of the kingdom of God (see Mosiah 15:10–11).

Knowing

One side of the religion triangle is *knowing*. This suggests the need for an understanding of the meaning of life. In gaining this understanding, one searches for answers to those oft-repeated questions: Where did I come from? Why am I here? and Where will I go after I die? Such answers are found as one searches the scriptures, hears the words of the prophets, ponders the revelations past and present, and prays for a knowledge of God and his holy purposes. In time, a theology or set of beliefs emerges, and Christ's doctrine is fitted together like a jigsaw puzzle.

Throughout your quest for knowledge of God and his dealings with men, bear in mind that a person cannot be saved in ignorance (see D&C 131:6), that whatever knowledge and intelligence is gained in this life will give one the advantage in the world to come (see D&C 130:18–19), and that it is life eternal to "know thee the only true God, and Jesus Christ, whom thou hast sent" (John 17:3).

Missionaries and Church members must engage themselves in the cognitive level of learning as they search the scriptures and listen to living prophets. One must press for a knowledge of facts, principles, laws, and saving ordinances related to the gospel of Christ. Once one has obtained for oneself a mental affirmation of the truthfulness of the message one bears, one can teach it with power and authority to others, keeping in mind this admonition: "Seek not to declare my word, but first seek to obtain my word, and then shall your tongue be loosed; then, if you desire, you shall have my Spirit and my word, yea, the power of God unto the convincing of men" (D&C 11:21).

Feeling

The other side of the religion triangle is *feeling*. This aspect of religion deals with the emotions, the things of the Spirit, or the so-called inner man. On occasions God speaks to us in our minds and hearts by the Holy Ghost (see D&C 8:2–3; 9:8). At other times he speaks peace to our minds concerning matters of great importance (see D&C 6:22–24). He even reveals truths by his Spirit in such a way that we can testify that we have heard his voice and know of his words (see Enos 1:10; D&C 18:34–36).

All of us have been endowed with a conscience, sometimes referred to as the light or "Spirit of Christ" (Moroni 7:16). Such power of feeling enables us to judge the goodness or badness of things so long as we live righteously. But if we sin and pollute our body, that power of feeling is numbed or lost completely, and we are left to our own resources. One weeps over those who drive the Spirit from their lives and who reach a state when they are "past feeling" (1 Nephi 17:45) because they lose contact with pure religion.

It is the feeling or spiritual side of the religion triangle that causes a person to embrace values and make commitments. Often we hear, "It is the Spirit that converts." Few will commit to be baptized unless they have received a spiritual experience or confirmation of the truth. Moreover, few will commit to keep the commandments and serve in the Church until they have received the Holy Ghost and allowed that special gift to show them what they should do (see 2 Nephi 32:1–5).

Those who desire to share the gospel must court the Holy Spirit and testify boldly to would-be listeners. In the process we provide others with emotional experiences that will touch hearts and result in a spiritual confirmation of truths spoken. Each lesson taught should be a spiritual experience—an edifying, affective learning experience—stirring emotions and causing throbs of the heart. Each step of repentance taken will draw us closer to Christ.

Doing

At the base of the religion triangle is *doing*. Whole books have been written on this subject. Perhaps the most quoted text is the book of James in the New Testament, wherein we are reminded that "faith without works is dead" (James 2:20).

The Savior himself taught, "My doctrine is not mine, but his that sent me. If any man will *do* his will, he shall know of the doctrine, whether it be of God, or whether I speak of myself." (John 7:16–17; emphasis added.) There is virtue in knowing something about God;

there is the thrill of feeling after the Spirit; but until one actually tests the doctrine by applying it to one's own life and circumstances, one really never experiences pure religion.

It should not be forgotten that we will be judged by our thoughts, words, and *deeds* (see Mosiah 4:29–30). There is not only sanctification and joy in the practice of full religion but also safety—safety for the soul.

Full or complete conversion does not occur until one has applied the things heard and felt. Words and emotions must be translated into actions; otherwise the blessings associated with laws and ordinances are forfeited.

In summary, it is accurate to say that the method used by true believers in sharing the gospel is nothing more nor less than the practice of pure religion and the invitation extended to others to do the same. Such an invitation is extended by teaching, testifying, and exemplifying so effectively that truth-seekers will want to come unto Christ by living the commandments and participating in saving ordinances. It should be remembered that one's effectiveness in sharing the gospel with others is dependent upon one's depth of knowledge, degree of spirituality, and consistency in modeling righteousness.

Traditional Approaches

This discussion of proselyting methods would be incomplete if something were not said about the traditional approaches to missionary service. I refer to the finding, friendshipping, teaching, baptizing, and fellowshipping activities that must be pursued continually and simultaneously.

Finding

Most members and missionaries agree that *finding* people to teach is the real challenge of missionary service. If you don't find, you don't teach; and if you don't teach, you don't convert. So the rub comes in scrambling for men and women who will listen to the message.

In a few places, the people seem eager and prepared to receive the missionaries. It is as if the elect have already been identified. But in other places hearts seem hard and doors remain closed. Such closed circumstances require diligence, patience, and ingenuity by those who have been given the commission to fish and hunt for the honest in heart (see Jeremiah 16:16).

The successful finders are those who see inherent goodness in others and view people not as they are but as they may become. They are not timid, nor are they socially unskilled. They grasp every opportunity to serve and to bless the lives of young and old alike. They go about doing good, following the model of the Sinless One whom they represent. Like the sons of Mosiah, they can say, "We have entered into their houses and taught them, and we have taught them in their streets; yea, and we have taught them upon their hills; and we have also entered into their temples and their synagogues and taught them" (Alma 26:29).

Friendshipping

Once an investigator is found, the next order of business is to establish strong bonds of friendship. This must be done very discreetly. Overfamiliarity or too much informality often undermines the image of the messenger and distracts the investigator. On the other hand, timidity or aloofness may cause the truth-seeker to doubt one's sincerity.

Without question, members are better equipped to friendship people than are missionaries. They are not subject to transfer from a place on short notice, nor are they restricted by the spartan rules that missionaries must obey. It should be remembered that many questions arise in the minds of nonmembers during the investigation process. No one is better qualified to address these questions than a member who resides close by and who has probably entertained the same concerns at one time or another.

The sooner an investigator attends church and becomes acquainted with the Saints, the greater his or her chances are of remaining steadfast in the quest for truth.

Teaching

Real teaching occurs when there is a heart-to-heart exchange of information under the influence of the Holy Ghost. It was Emerson who said: "The same reality pervades all teaching. The man may teach by doing, and not otherwise. If he can communicate himself, he can teach, but not by words. He teaches who gives, and he learns who receives. There is no teaching until the pupil is brought into the same state or principal in which you are; a transfusion takes place; he is you, and you are he; then is . . . teaching." (*The Works of Ralph Waldo Emerson* [Roslyn, New York: Black's Readers Service Co., n.d.], p. 135.)

The transfusion of truth and testimony is facilitated when the actions of teachers confirm the spoken word. Such transfusion begins when the missionary or member addresses the listener in the spirit of truth and with a clear eye. It progresses as pure motive is revealed and honest testimony is shared. It culminates when commitments are drawn and behavior is made to conform with the principles of the gospel of Jesus Christ, as modeled by the messenger.

In the early years of the restored Church, the Lord commanded, "Ye shall instruct and edify each other" (D&C 43:8). *Instruct* means to inform or share information, with or without the Spirit. *Edify,* however, means to inspire or to build morally—something that will occur only under the influence of the Holy Spirit. Therefore, all teaching, whether provided by members or missionaries, must be instructive and edifying to all truth-seekers.

Baptizing

If anyone questions the importance of baptism, that person should read again the holy scriptures. Not only does the word of God remind us that repentance and baptism constitute the gate to the strait and narrow path leading to eternal life, it also reminds us that it is the means by which entrance into the kingdom of God is obtained. Christ himself was baptized "to fulfil all righteousness," to set an example, and to demonstrate his willingness to keep the commandments of the Father. Therefore, all must be taught and invited to participate in this saving ordinance. (See 2 Nephi 31; 3 Nephi 11.)

All that is said and done by members and missionaries should be pointed toward the baptism of worthy candidates—

- Who have repented and "brought forth fruit meet that they [are] worthy of [baptism]."
- Who "[come] forth with a broken heart and a contrite spirit."

- Who have "witnessed unto the church that they [have] truly repented of all their sins."
- Who are willing to take upon them "the name of Christ, having a determination to serve him to the end." (Moroni 6:1–3.)

Fellowshipping

Fellowshipping is a process that relates to all Church members, organizations, and programs. It requires the development of a genuine spirit of love and mutual concern among members. It includes efforts that result in a newly baptized person becoming actively engaged in building experiences with the Saints. It implies social contact, activities, service opportunities, and worship services that strengthen testimony and expedite integration into "the body of Christ" (1 Corinthians 12:27).

"For," as Paul wrote, "the body is not one member, but many. . . . And whether one member suffer, all the members suffer with it; or one member be honoured, all the members rejoice with it." (1 Corinthians 12:14, 26.)

Toward the end of the Book of Mormon, Moroni describes fellowshipping: "And after they had been received unto baptism, and were wrought upon and cleansed by the power of the Holy Ghost, they were numbered among the people of the church of Christ; and their names were taken, that they might be remembered and nourished by the good word of God, to keep them in the right way, to keep them continually watchful unto prayer, relying alone upon the merits of Christ, who was the author and the finisher of their faith. And the church did meet together oft, to fast and to pray, and to speak one with another concerning the welfare of their souls." (Moroni 6:4–5.)

Many times the Lord has likened missionary service to the harvesting of a crop. He has announced that the field is ripe and that the reapers should thrust in their sickles and work with all their might. But it has been emphasized that the labor is not finished until the sheaves are gathered safely into the garners so that nothing is wasted. No convert can be considered as fully gathered into the garner and in the hands of the Lord of the Harvest until he has been fellowshipped and changed from a stranger to God to a fellowcitizen with the Saints. (See Alma 26:4–7; Ephesians 2:19.)

Waterwheel Analogy

The cyclical process of finding, friendshipping, teaching, baptizing, and fellowshipping may be likened to the work of a waterwheel used to lift water from a lower to a higher level of ground. First, buckets on the rim of the wheel scoop up the water from the flowing stream. Such action of the wheel may be compared to the finding and friendshipping efforts of members and missionaries, who search and fish the stream of humanity for people who are interested in hearing their message. Second, once the water is in the bucket, the force of the running stream pushes the loaded buckets upward, even though there is some spillage caused by the movement of the wheel. Similarly, missionaries and members teach and friendship investigators as they accept the truth and make needed improvements in their way of living. Great efforts are made to prevent dropouts and spillage of contacts during this critical upward climb. Third, when the buckets full of water reach the top of the wheel, they are tripped, causing the water to flow freely into the higher channel. This action represents baptism in the proselyting cycle. At this point of conversion, the investigator enters the waters of baptism worthily and joins the body of Saints. Finally, just as the water is cared for in the higher channel by the water master, so is the newly baptized member watched over and fellowshipped by those who want their fruits to remain.

Gospel Invitations and Commitments

The saving process in which members and missionaries participate is described by President Joseph Fielding Smith in a pit and ladder analogy:

A man walking along the road happens to fall into a pit so deep and dark that he cannot climb to the surface and regain his freedom. How can he save himself from his predicament? Not by any exertions on his part, for there is no means of escape in the pit. He calls for help and some kindly disposed soul, hearing his cries for relief, hastens to his assistance and by lowering a ladder, gives to him the means by which he may climb again to the surface of the earth.

This was precisely the condition that Adam placed himself and his posterity in, when he partook of the forbidden fruit. All being together in the pit, none could gain the surface and relieve the others. The pit was banishment from the presence of the Lord and temporal death, the dissolution of the body. And all being subject to death, none could provide the means of escape.

Therefore, in his infinite mercy, the Father heard the cries of his children and sent his Only Begotten Son, who was not subject to death nor to sin, to provide the means of escape. This he did through his infinite atonement and the everlasting gospel. (*Doctrines of Salvation*, comp. Bruce R. McConkie, 3 vols. [Salt Lake City: Book-craft, 1954], 1:126–27.)

In President Smith's story, the man who fell into the pit represents all of us who, as a consequence of the fall of Adam, live in mortality. The pit represents the world in which we live—a place of temptation, sin, and error. The ladder represents Christ's atonement and everlasting gospel, or the means by which men and women gain their freedom from physical and spiritual death. The man who lowers the ladder represents the Savior—he who was sent by the Father to redeem mankind. The surface of the earth represents the presence of God, where only the righteous dwell.

Application

This pit and ladder analogy may be applied to the proselyting service that members and missionaries render. We have already accepted Christ and climbed the ladder out of the pit of sinners. Now, in behalf of the Savior, we invite others to believe in Christ, to repent, to take advantage of the Atonement, and to embrace the everlasting gospel with its saving principles and ordinances. We do all of this and more knowing that it is a special honor to represent the Savior.

People do not move out of the pit of sinners into the body of the Saints in one giant leap. Such movement includes the wholehearted acceptance of the invitation to come unto Christ and the ascension step by step from the darkness of the pit to the light of the surface, where the righteous dwell.

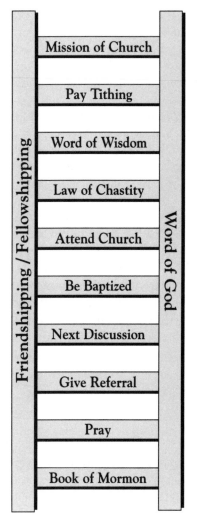

As the Prophet Joseph Smith taught: "When you climb up a ladder, you must begin at the bottom, and ascend step by step, until you arrive at the top; and so it is with the principles of the Gospel—you must begin with the first, and go on until you learn all the principles of exaltation" (*Teachings of the Prophet Joseph Smith*, comp. Joseph Fielding Smith [Salt Lake City: Deseret Book Co., 1977], p. 348).

Just as the Lord gives to us line upon line and precept upon precept as we lend an ear to his counsel, so must believers invite nonbelievers to move rung by rung Godward as they respond to gospel teachings (see 2 Nephi 28:30).

We must keep in mind that each rung on the ladder is essential and should not be ignored by those concerned. Otherwise something is lost in the change process, and in the end the conversion is incomplete.

The first invitation may be to *read the Book of Mormon*. Once an investigator has committed to do this, he or she may be invited to *pray* about the book. And on and on it goes invitation by invitation and commitment by commitment up the gospel ladder. Remember, each step is vital. Each step helps to bring the sinner's "soul from the pit, to be enlightened with the light of the living" (Job 33:30). For example:

— If an investigator is invited to *give a referral* and does so, he or she becomes a member of our team and a part of our saving effort and is more committed to the teaching process.

—When an investigator agrees to *hear the next discussion,* he or she is much more inclined to read the Book of Mormon and pray about it.

—Once we invite a person to *be baptized* and *attend church* and he or she commits, the Spirit grows stronger and the progress of the individual is accelerated.

—The same applies to *living the law of chastity, living the word of wisdom,* and *paying tithing.* All must be invited to live these laws, and all must commit themselves to live them, just as they have been taught. If not, needed adjustments in lifestyle are not made and the investigator falls back into the pit.

—Last but not least of the commitments is related to the promise to *actively take part in fulfilling the mission of the Church.* This commitment must not be approached casually, for it is service that distinguishes the righteous from the wicked (3 Nephi 24:18). It is service that clinches the conversion.

Ladders have two handrails. These rails not only give strength to the ladder itself but also enable the climber to maintain balance and direction as he or she puts one foot above the other. One rail of the gospel ladder is the word of God. So long as the investigator clings to the scriptures, particularly the Book of Mormon, and presses upward and forward, nothing will impede his or her progress. The investigator will be able to withstand the scoffings of so-called friends, the pressures from family members, the lies and half-truths about the Church circulated by misinformed individuals, and other negative influences or mists of darkness that would block his way (see 1 Nephi 8:24). As we sing in one of our hymns, "Hold to the rod, the iron rod; 'tis strong, and bright, and true. The iron rod is the word of God; 'twill safely guide us through." (Joseph L. Townsend, "The Iron Rod," in *Hymns,* no. 274.)

Speaking of the latter days, the remnant of his seed, and the scriptures compiled by his people, Nephi said: "Wherefore, they shall come to the knowledge of their Redeemer and the very points of his doctrine, that they may know *how to come unto him* and be saved" (1 Nephi 15:14; emphasis added). This statement and many others found within the Book of Mormon teach us that the book is a *how-to* book. It teaches us how to come unto Christ.

Therefore, we must get our investigators into the Book of Mormon as soon as we can. We must keep their hands upon this rail throughout the conversion process. We should refer to the latter-day scriptures in each discussion. We should permit spiritual giants like Nephi, Alma, Mormon, and others to assist us in bearing testimony of Christ. We should encourage our contacts to seek answers to their doctrinal questions from the writings of Lehi, Jacob, Moroni, and others. We should read to our investigators and invite them to read selected passages from the Book of Mormon to us. In the process, their grip on the rail will grow firmer and firmer, and their resolve to climb all the way out of the pit will become stronger and stronger.

The other rail of the ladder is friendshipping and fellowshipping with stalwart members of the Church. We cannot place the hands of our investigators into the hands of members too soon. I say this because it is the members who help our contacts feel that they are "no more strangers and foreigners, but fellowcitizens with the saints, and of the household of God" (Ephesians 2:19). It is the Church organization and members who help prevent investigators from being "tossed to and fro, and carried about with every wind of doctrine" (Ephesians 4:14).

In hearing our discussions, reading the Book of Mormon, and praying about our invitations, the investigator undergoes an intellectual and spiritual conversion. However, the much-needed social conversion comes through the members of the Church who extend the hand of fellowship. Studies show that the drop-off rate of investigators is much, much lower when nonmembers climb the ladder of the gospel hand in hand with members of the Church. Of one couple it was said: "Their choice [was] made, and they turn[ed] away hand-in-hand, with their backs to the darkness [pit of sinners] and their faces to the light [heavenward]" (Arthur Conan Doyle, *The White Company* [New York: Cosmopolitan Book Corp., 1922], p. 361). This is the vision that we must retain in our minds. In our mind's eye we must see each prospective member climbing up the gospel ladder with his or her hand clasped in the hand of a member who shows the way.

Missionaries come and go. They are sent into a city or area for a few months, and then they are transferred. Therefore it is imperative that the hands of investigators are placed upon the rails of the gospel ladder. The iron rod of the scriptures remains after the missionary goes. The members continue to live in the city even though the missionary goes elsewhere. It is the scriptures and the members that provide the repentant person stability in his or her climb out of the pit. Moreover, these rails lend encouragement to those who question whether the struggle is worthwhile. They also hold up and steady those who may stumble along the way.

There is a little saving virtue in each single rung on the ladder. However, the prospects of eternal life require the investigator to take more than just one step upward. Eternal life or God's life will come only to those who escape the pit. Therefore, we must be diligent in our service and do all within our power to help people climb the ladder all the way to the top. Yes, it should be our desire to obtain many fruits from our labors, but it should also be our desire to see that our fruits remain (see John 15:16).

Christ not only taught the saving principles and ordinances of the gospel, but he also lived and died for us. Thus he extends to all mankind the precious gifts of immortality and eternal life.

The free gift of immortality will be received by all who live upon this earth, regardless of whether or not they climb the gospel ladder and escape the pit of sinners. However, only those who climb step by step up the gospel ladder will obtain the gift of eternal life. As agents of Deity, we lower the ladder into the pit and extend the divine invitation.

There is a scripture that reads: "[Jacob] dreamed, and behold a ladder set up on the earth, and the top of it reached to heaven: and behold the angels of God ascending and descending on it" (Genesis 28:12). I love the symbolism of this verse of scripture.

According to President Marion G. Romney, Jacob realized "that the covenants he there made with the Lord were the rungs on the ladder which he himself would have to climb in order to obtain the promised blessings—blessings that would entitle him to enter heaven and associate with the Lord" (*Look to God and Live*, comp. George J. Romney [Salt Lake City: Deseret Book Co., 1971], p. 240).

Of those members and missionaries who act as agents of the Lord and assist others in escaping the pit, it will be said:

—"He brought me up also out of an horrible pit, out of the miry clay, and set my feet upon a rock, and established my goings" (Psalm 40:2).

—"Thou hast in love to my soul delivered it from the pit of corruption: for thou hast cast all my sins behind thy back" (Isaiah 38:17).

"Thank You for Lifting Us Up"

On one occasion I requested an elder to report to the mission home for a final interview and a farewell testimonial. He had been a faithful servant—one who had converted more than a few people during his two years of service. After receiving my notice, he called me on the telephone wondering if it would be all right for a couple he had recently brought into the Church to drive him to the mission office. I did not object as long as it was not an inconvenience or imposition to the man and his wife.

At the appointed day and hour, the missionary and his new converts arrived. I met them at the door and quickly observed the special love that existed between the missionary and the couple with whom he had shared the gospel. They talked and talked, as if both parties were loathe to say good-bye. Finally I reminded the little group that my time was limited and that we must proceed with the interview.

With tears in his eyes, the missionary shook hands with the couple and said: "Thanks so very much for bringing me down to Dallas." Very quickly the man responded in a quivering voice, "No, Elder, *thank you for lifting us up.*"

Missionary service is summarized beautifully in this one sentence—"Thank you for lifting us up." "Thank you for lifting us up from the pit of sin and helping us to come unto Christ."

As God has planted a portion of His Spirit within [mankind], He will hold them, and not us, responsible for their acts. . . . Honorable men cannot condescend to chicanery and deception; and while following the lead of that inward monitor, they could not yield themselves to those heartless and cold-blooded practices. . . . Noah had nothing to do but to preach the Gospel, and obey the word of the Lord. We have nothing to do but attend to the same things. We then leave the inhabitants of the earth in the hands of God. . . . I would not use any influence but that of truth to lead any man to a knowledge of the truth. Any other influence, any other power, any other spirit is not of God. (John Taylor, in Journal of Discourses *24:290, 292.)*

6

MOTIVATION

"Motivation That Comes of True Conversion"

As we work with [people] there is much more to be achieved than statistical improvement. Such improvement is, of course, desirable, and must be worked for. But, more importantly, we should be concerned with the spiritual dimension of our people and the enlargement of this dimension. There is a tendency in all of us to ask for better statistical performance. There is a tendency to impose quotas behind which usually lies imposition of pressure to achieve improved statistics. In the work of the Lord there is a more appropriate motivation than pressure. There is the motivation that comes of true conversion. When there are throbs in the heart of an individual Latter-day Saint, a great and vital testimony of the truth of this work, he will be found doing his duty in the Church. . . . He will have within him a great desire to share the gospel with others. He will be found strengthening and lifting his brethren and sisters. It is conversion that makes the difference. (President Gordon B. Hinckley, Regional Representatives Seminar, 6 April 1984.)

The sixth M of missionary service is motivation—that spiritual nudging that comes from within, causing people to bestir themselves and "to be up and doing" (see Alma 60:24, 29).

Conversion made a difference in the life of Enos, a Book of Mormon personality. We do not know much about the man prior to his wrestle before God. We do know, however, that he reached a point in his life when his "soul hungered" and he prayed to his Maker all the day long and into the night. In the end, his faith and pleadings were rewarded, for he heard a voice declare, "Thy sins are forgiven thee, and thou shalt be blessed." (See Enos 1:1–8.)

Once Enos had received a remission of his sins, a remarkable and significant change came over him. He said, "I began to feel a desire for the welfare of my brethren, the Nephites." But that was not all! His heartfelt desires extended beyond his own people to his enemies, and he prayed earnestly for them also. (See Enos 1:9–11.)

Enos's case is not unusual. It seems that deeply spiritual experiences sweep self-centered concerns aside and replace them with concerns for others. Once Lehi had tasted a fruit desirable to make one happy, he wanted his family to partake of it also. Once Alma had received the inspiring report from his missionary friends, he wanted to be an angel so that he could declare repentance to every people. When converted, Enos, Lehi, and Alma were filled with desires for others and became highly motivated messengers of the Lord. (See 1 Nephi 8:11–12; Alma 29:1–2.)

Motive and Desire

Motive and desire seem to be closely related, especially in matters pertaining to sharing the gospel. A motive is defined as something within a person such as a need, idea, or emotion that incites him or her to action. Desire is a longing for or a craving to be or to do something.

The need for forgiveness of sins caused Enos to pray; the idea or prospects of eternal life caused a king to offer all that he possessed (see Alma 22:15); and love of the Lord caused Mary to pour precious ointment upon the head of Jesus (see Matthew 26:6–13). All three possessed a motivation born of true conversion. Each had a longing in his heart for the welfare of others. Each had received a spiritual manifestation of the reality of God and the importance of his work. And each had the "throbs in the heart" spoken of by President Gordon B. Hinckley.

Pure Motive and Real Intent

Two other related expressions are worthy of comment in this discussion: *pure motive* and *real intent*. Both expressions are defined as the urge to do the right thing at the right time and for the right reason.

The angel Moroni warned the Prophet Joseph Smith that he "must have no other object in view in getting the plates but to *glorify* God, and must not be influenced by any other *motive* than that of *building his kingdom*" (Joseph Smith—History 1:46; emphasis added). Without purity of motive, Joseph might have been drawn into behavior similar to priestcraft (see 2 Nephi 26:29) and may have become like King Amaziah, who "did that which was right in the sight of the Lord, but not with a perfect heart" (2 Chronicles 25:2).

Elder Dallin H. Oaks wrote about the need to do things in the Lord's way. In a chapter on motive and real intent, he stated:

> The contrast between the motive to help and the motive to use can even be seen in some Church service. A missionary with a motive to use "his" mission for personal growth and "his" baptisms to gain recognition for "his" accomplishments is a phony and a failure. His motives and attitudes are transparent. Companions, leaders, and investigators will soon recognize and resent a missionary who sees them as mere objects to be used for his benefit.
>
> A missionary who sees himself (or herself) as a servant of the Lord, an instrument in his hands to do his work (Alma 17:9), has the motive to *help* others. That attitude and motive is transparent also, and its fruits are trust and love from all with whom the missionary associates. (*Pure in Heart* [Salt Lake City: Bookcraft, 1988], p. 30; emphasis in original.)

At a regional conference I heard Elder Oaks say, "A missionary who concentrates upon what he can *give* is usually much more effective than one who concentrates upon what he can *get* or receive." The same could be said of members who invite others to come unto Christ.

Mormon taught: "A man being evil cannot do that which is good; for if he offereth a gift, or prayeth unto God, except he shall do it with *real intent* it profiteth him nothing" (Moroni 7:6; emphasis added).

All members and missionaries, in their efforts to share the gospel, must understand that pure motive, full purpose of heart, and real intent win the approbation of God and unleash the powers of self and the Spirit. Selfish and phony approaches used by messengers are actually satanic and betray the message given.

Forms of Motivation

It would be very nice if all members of the Church possessed the desire, will, motive, and real intent to preach Christ and him crucified. But such is not the case. A few are self-starters and move forward on their own. Many, however, require some encouragement before they will participate in certain things. Hence, in the Church there is a place for motivators—people who stir emotions and excite feelings in others, causing them to act in a certain way. One may motivate by lending encouragement; another may motivate with a smile, a handshake, a nod of the head, or some other gesture of approval; still others use incentives, songs, conversion stories, inspiring statements, testimonies, and a variety of approaches to release the driving power found within an individual. Leaders do not invent the motivation; they simply assist others in unlocking and expressing what is already there, however deeply it may be hidden.

All of us have been exposed to leaders who employed various motivational tactics—some honorable and some not so honorable.

Fear Motivation

I once played for a coach who believed that fear motivation worked best. He would shout threats to the players, shower them with intimidating remarks, and goad them toward a higher level of performance with offensive profanity. Some have been exposed to shades of fear motivation in the military, where the officer's expression of so-called tough love was intended to make soldiers walk faster and shoot straighter.

I suppose that fear motivation was employed to an extent at the time of Ananias and Sapphira. This couple lied to the Lord and lost their lives. Of those who witnessed their deaths, we read: "Great fear came on all them that heard these things" (Acts 5:5).

Sometimes fear provokes this kind of a resolve: "[I will] work out [my] own salvation with fear and trembling" (Philippians 2:12). However, fear motivation has its problems. Apathy often returns when the threat is removed; it can be applied in a devilish way; and it is often applied in a way contrary to the manner in which the power and influence of the priesthood is maintained (see D&C 121:41–46).

In my mind, the use of fear or threat is the lowest and least desirable form of motivation. It is imposed to intimidate and to keep a person going against his or her will. Heavy-handed tactics by leaders are always suspect and have limited, if any, place in the Lord's program. The use of fear motivation in sharing the gospel is too much like meeting a would-be believer with the scriptures in one hand and a club in the other.

Reward Motivation

Reward or "carrot" motivation is a common form used with children. This approach usually centers around expected rewards, such as money, medals, badges, certificates, trophies, and other tangible enticements. Perhaps this motivational approach has its place, but it also has its drawbacks, including: the carrot must get progressively bigger to sustain its appeal; the promised reward can cause people to do things for the wrong reason; and this approach tends to focus the recipient's mind upon himself or herself rather than upon Christ and the proselyting work.

But this type of motivation becomes less suspect when the reward or promise involved is intangible or spiritual in nature. For example, the Lord revealed a law of health that we call the Word of Wisdom. Among other things, God said: "And all saints who remember to keep and do these sayings, walking in obedience to the commandments, *shall receive*" (D&C 89:18; emphasis added). After all, we read in the scriptures, "I, the Lord, am bound when ye do what I say; but when ye do not what I say, ye have no promise [or reward]" (D&C 82:10). What is wrong with keeping a commandment with the promised blessings in mind to sustain one's resolve?

We hope that the "what's in it for me" attitude would become more and more subliminal as the person sharing the gospel gains maturity, becomes acquainted with pure motive, and loses himself or herself in selfless service.

The Lord said, "But when thou doest alms, let not thy left hand know what thy right hand doeth: that thine alms may be in secret" (Matthew 6:3–4). Those who strive to share the gospel with the hope of some tangible reward uppermost in their minds are too much like those who give with one hand and expect to receive with the other or who give a gift that sticks to their fingers. On the other hand, those who give or share with an intangible blessing in mind are required to exercise a greater faith. Their motive for doing seems purer than those who do with the expectation of an immediate and tangible return.

Sense of Duty Motivation

Another form of motivation is referred to as the sense of duty approach. This form presupposes that a person has a lively con-science, is willing to learn his or her duty, and possesses the moral in-tegrity to act accordingly.

We have a scriptural injunction: "Let us hear the conclusion of the whole matter: Fear God, and keep his commandments: for this is the whole duty of man" (Ecclesiastes 12:13). Moreover, we read re-solves such as the one voiced by Jonah: "But I will sacrifice unto thee with the voice of thanksgiving; I will pay that that I have vowed" (Jonah 2:9).

No one will deny the need and the importance of the missionary or member understanding the special commission that he or she has been given and serving accordingly. The call comes from the Lord through a living prophet, along with this expectation: "Let every man learn his duty, and to act in the office in which he is appointed, in all diligence" (D&C 107:99).

Fear motivation may have a limited place in the missionary pro-gram of the Church. We would not fault anyone for praying as Nephi prayed, "O Lord, . . . wilt thou make me that I may shake at the ap-pearance of sin?" (2 Nephi 4:31.) Nor would we condemn any who served with the hope of receiving the full blessings or rewards associ-ated with valiant missionary service, including a forgiveness of sins (see D&C 62:3). And we certainly would not criticize anyone who serves dutifully with the desire of fulfilling divine expectations (see Jacob 1:17–19).

Spiritual or Inner Motivation

But is all of that enough? Is there not a form of motivation that is higher and more desirable than fear, reward, or sense of duty? The an-swer to this question is an emphatic yes. There is an inner motiva-tion—the ultimate form of motivation that has spiritual dimensions, comes of true conversion, and is spurred by throbs in the heart.

I believe that something Elder Boyd K. Packer taught in a conference address applies to the higher form of motivation. He said, "True doctrine, understood, changes attitudes and behavior. The study of the doctrines of the gospel will improve behavior quicker than a study of behavior will improve behavior. . . . That is why we stress so forcefully the study of the doctrines of the gospel." (In Conference Report, October 1986, p. 20.)

Elder Packer's words lead us to spiritual or inner-directed motivation—a motivation rooted in the gospel of Jesus Christ and built upon the foundation of truth. It begins with faith, grows with knowledge, and results in a compelling desire to act. Such motivation is void of fear, does not offend agency, and does not feed upon enticements of external rewards; rather, it rallies the sacred powers within one's soul.

As mentioned earlier, Alma cried, "O that I were an angel, and could have the wish of mine heart, that I might go forth and speak with the trump of God, with a voice to shake the earth, and cry repentance unto every people!" (Alma 29:1.) Moreover, he said: "I know that he granteth unto men according to their desire . . . ; yea, I know that he allotteth unto men . . . according to their *wills*" (Alma 29:4; emphasis added). Alma's motivation was not born of fear, focused upon reward, or controlled by a sense of duty. It was a powerful feeling surging from the center of his soul, causing him "to perform the work to which I have been called" (Alma 29:6) and to "be an instrument in the hands of God to bring some soul to repentance" (Alma 29:9).

Gospel-Rooted Concepts of Men

Over the years some Church leaders, including mission presidents, have used motivational ideas gleaned from a variety of sources. They have used tapes, records, films, and self-helps produced by success and motivational experts in the business world. More than a few have used materials found in books such as *The Greatest Salesman in the World*, *Think and Grow Rich*, and similar sources. All of them provide approaches to purposeful and effective living but must be used judiciously, if at all, by those who have been commissioned to go into the world and teach all nations (see Matthew 28:19–20).

We should understand clearly that motivational information

produced and peddled by institutes and individuals is simply attempts by people to lead others, particularly salespeople, toward greater heights of achievement. They must not be accepted as foolproof systems, nor should they be substituted for a person's religion or priesthood mandate.

Perhaps we may justify the use of commercial success and motivation materials as learning aids. For example, we frequently quote a poet or writer to illustrate a truth cited in the Bible or Book of Mormon. In a similar way, we may refer to motivational concepts used in the business world to help us apply gospel truths more effectively. After all, we do say to the world: "If there is anything virtuous, lovely, or of good report or praiseworthy, we seek after these things" (Articles of Faith 1:13). If virtuous or praiseworthy materials are found in the world, is it wrong to use them? The answer is no, providing, of course, that we realize their limitation and do not allow them to replace the scriptures or the instructions of our Church leaders.

Several years ago, when I was involved with the Missionary Department of the Church, I collected the most popular motivational programs and materials on the market and listened to tapes produced by Earl Nightingale, Zig Ziglar, Bob Richards, and others. My investigation may not have been exhaustive, but it was sufficient for me to reach this conclusion: The great motivators of the day are teaching nothing more or less than gospel truths clothed in common, ordinary language. In fact, almost every book written and every talk given by these much-hyped artists centers on four basic concepts: a healthy self-image, a positive mental attitude, goal-oriented action, and high standards and expectations.

These four concepts—a healthy self-image, a positive mental attitude, goal-oriented action, and high standards and expectations—are really basic gospel principles, rooted deeply in the teachings of Jesus Christ. Those who have discovered the value of these simple but powerful truths and who have produced motivational programs based upon gospel concepts are actually marketing a portion of the Master's way of life.

A Healthy Self-Image

Self-image is really an individual's mental and spiritual picture of himself or herself. Many regard self-image as the strongest force within a person. It is the product of what a person knows, thinks, and experiences.

If self-image or self-esteem is low, personal conduct and performance are generally low. On the other hand, if one's self-concept is enhanced, personality and behavior are usually enhanced. There is truth in the line, "For as he thinketh in his heart, so is he" (Proverbs 23:7).

Maxwell Maltz wrote: "The word 'esteem' literally means to appreciate the worth of. Why do men stand in awe of the stars, and the moon, the immensity of the sea, the beauty of a flower or a sunset, and at the same time downgrade themselves? Did not the same Creator make man? Is not man himself the most marvelous creation of all? This appreciation of your own worth is not egotism unless you assume that you made yourself and should take some of the credit. . . . For real self-esteem is not derived from the great things you've done, the things you own, the mark you've made—but an appreciation of yourself for what you *are—a child of God.*" (*Psycho-Cybernetics* [Englewood Cliffs, New Jersey: Prentice-Hall, 1969], pp. 121–22; emphasis added.)

A Positive Mental Attitude

A positive mental attitude is really the result of faith and repentance. If a person has faith in himself or herself and God, he or she discards self-limiting thoughts, such as "I can't do it." If a person repents from past transgression, he or she pushes aside encumbering thoughts, such as "I'm not worthy."

Feelings and thoughts go hand in hand. One who suffers with a low self-image is prone to engage in what Zig Ziglar calls "stinkin' thinkin'." He or she sees the glass half-empty rather than half-full. He or she cites readily all the reasons why something cannot be done. He or she habitually looks for shadows and anticipates defeat.

Dr. Maltz wrote: "The unhappiest mortal is that man who incites upon relieving the past, over and over in his imagination—continually criticizing himself for past sins. . . . The minute that we change our minds, and stop giving power to the past, the past with its mistakes loses power over us." (*Psycho-Cybernetics*, pp. 66–67.)

Too many people dissipate their strength by wallowing in the muck of the past. They fetter themselves with a type of double mindedness that James said makes a person "unstable in all his ways" (James 1:8). Only through the exercise of faith and genuine repentance can a person cut the cords of the past, purify his or her heart, and obtain power through a positive mental attitude.

To those who bring forth fruit meet for repentance, God grants forgiveness (see Alma 12:15). This forgiveness includes a sweeping of the mind and the putting on of the "new man" (Colossians 3:10). The new man, if repentance is complete, will be armed with a "willing mind" and "a readiness to will" (2 Corinthians 8:11–12).

"Let virtue garnish thy thoughts unceasingly," said the Lord; "then shall *thy confidence wax strong in the presence of God;* and the doctrine of the priesthood shall distil upon thy soul as the dews from heaven. The Holy Ghost shall be thy constant companion, and thy scepter an unchanging scepter of righteousness and truth." (D&C 121:45–46; emphasis added.)

The way we think and the thoughts we entertain can bless or condemn us (see Alma 12:14). Therefore, those who share the gospel must not allow their minds to harbor negative thoughts such as discouragement, fear, or doubt. Rather, they must gird up their loins and press forward, believing "I can do all things through Christ which strengtheneth me" (Philippians 4:13).

Goal-Oriented Action

President Spencer W. Kimball taught us: "To be sure your life will be full and abundant, you must plan your life" (in Conference Report, April 1974, p. 125).

Elder Thomas S. Monson gave this instruction: "Without a *goal* there can be no real success. Indeed, a good definition of success is: 'The progressive realization of a worthy ideal.'" (*Pathway to Perfection* [Salt Lake City: Deseret Book Co., 1973], p. 112; emphasis added.)

In harmony with the above teachings of inspired Church leaders, a motivational writer by the name of Ward Cantrell said: "Apathy can be overcome only by enthusiasm, and enthusiasm can be aroused by only two things: (1) an ideal (purpose) that takes the imagination by storm; and (b) a definite intelligible plan for carrying that ideal into practice. Set yourself a goal that you just have to reach. Then build the fire of anticipation under it. That goal will keep beckoning, and when you reach it, new goals will succeed to another."

We should remember that God himself has an avowed purpose or goal and a plan for accomplishing that purpose (see Moses 1:39). Moreover, he will not fail in his effort, for "there is nothing that the Lord thy God shall take in his heart to do but what he will do it" (Abraham 3:17).

Elder Gordon B. Hinckley taught: "Robert Browning said, 'A man's reach should exceed his grasp.' Growth comes as we constantly seek to achieve that which is just beyond our immediate capacity. One of the noteworthy aspects of the Church program is that it constantly motivates men to stretch themselves, to reach a little higher." (In Conference Report, April 1972, p. 77.)

Impure motives or selfish desires must not be reflected in goals. Goals must not be too rigid, approached in a mechanistic manner, or allowed to push aside inspiration of the moment. Goals must not be set as a means of forcing divine will or offending human agency. Yet if goals are to serve a purpose, they must be personal, challenging, and clearly understood.

I have long contended that someone without worthy goals becomes a pawn of time or circumstances. But with proper goals, that someone becomes the captain of his or her own destiny, providing he or she keeps in mind the injunction "Thy will be done" (Matthew 6:10) and remembers that God gives the increase (1 Corinthians 3:6).

High Standards and Expectations

A few wonder why Church standards are so high and why expectations are so great. They fail to understand that "one of the greatest blessings of life is law. . . . Without law, commandments, standards, and discipline, we would be utterly loose and utterly lost." (Richard L. Evans, *Thoughts for One Hundred Days*, vol. 4 [Salt Lake City: Publishers Press, 1970], pp. 143–44.) Followers of Christ are expected to do things "according to the will of the Lord" (D&C 64:29) and to live worthy of the companionship of the Holy Spirit. High expectations and willing obedience spur them on to greater heights of achievement and set them apart from others in the world. It is conceivable that Goethe had this thought in mind when he said: "If you treat a man as he is, he will remain as he is, but if you treat him as if he were what he ought to be, and could be, he will become what he ought to be, and should be" (quoted in Stan and Sharon Miller, *Especially for Mormons*, vol. 2 [Provo, Utah: Kellirae Arts, 1973], p. 209).

Someone has written, "The high expectations of others may even help motivate us or encourage us to reach heights we otherwise would not even attempt to strive for." However, "When we begin to be motivated by what we think is best . . . then we begin to make our own decisions," and self-motivation takes over. ("What Other People Think," *Church News*, 19 May 1990, p. 16.)

I do not fault the men and women of the world who teach and sell motivational programs based on gospel concepts. Rather, I applaud them for helping others understand the importance of a healthy self-image, a positive mental attitude, goal-oriented actions, and high standards and expectations. All of these aspects of motivation are virtuous when applied properly in one's life.

However, I would feel better about the professional motivators of the world if they would acknowledge openly the true author of their ideas and give him the credit due. If such acknowledgement were made, perhaps more would develop faith in the Master Motivator, who is the author and finisher of our faith. With such an increase of faith, more people, including members and missionaries, would be led toward the spiritual or inner motivation that comes with true conversion.

Spiritual Motivation—A Matter of Faith

"In all that we do," said President Gordon B. Hinckley, "we must cultivate faith. Increased faith is the touchstone to improved church performance." ("Missionary Service, Activation, Temple Work Emphasized in Conference Leadership Meetings," *Ensign*, May 1984, p. 99.)

Add to the above thoughts this statement by Elder James E. Talmage regarding the motive principle of faith: "In its broad sense, faith . . . is the motive principle that impels men to resolve and to act. Without its exercise, we would make no exertion the results of which are future. . . . Remove man's faith in the possibility of any desired success, and you rob him of the incentive to strive. He would not stretch forth his hand to seize did he not believe in the possibility of securing that for which he reaches. This principle becomes therefore the impelling force by which men struggle for excellence, ofttimes enduring vicissitudes and suffering that they may achieve their purposes. *Faith is the secret of ambition, the soul of heroism, the motive power of effort.*" (*The Articles of Faith,* 12th ed. [Salt Lake City: The Church of Jesus Christ of Latter-day Saints, 1924], pp. 102–3; emphasis added.)

Knowing what we know about the improvement of behavior through a study of the doctrines of the gospel, and knowing what we know about faith as "the motive power of effort," the question is: What can we do to motivate ourselves and others to share the gospel with more enthusiasm and consistency?

I propose that the genesis of self- or inner motivation is *faith*— faith in one's own self, faith in one's God, faith in one's cause, and faith in one's leaders.

Build Faith in Oneself

A follower of Christ who knows that he or she is the "offspring of God" (Acts 17:29), that he or she was made "a little lower than the angels," and that God has "crowned him with glory and honour" (see Psalm 8:3–6) will certainly have a stronger desire to be up and doing than one who regards himself or herself as merely an accident of nature.

Those who allow the mirror of self to become clouded, scratched, and hardly observable will be reluctant to share anything with others. However, those who possess faith in themselves will be more inclined to become anxiously engaged in the Lord's work. Therefore, it is important that we know who we are and what we are capable of doing and becoming by searching the scriptures and adding to our faith.

Elder Marion D. Hanks taught: "If one is to learn the answers to the basic spiritual problems of his life and is to pursue a purposeful program fruitfully and happily, he must have a motivation, an 'inner aim' our friends sometimes call it, a spiritual assurance, a testimony which will inspire and impell him to learn and to live" (in Conference Report, April 1956, p. 100).

This "inner aim" spoken of by Elder Hanks that inspires or impels someone to learn, live, and share is really a product of faith—faith in oneself. When someone is prompted to pray, "Lord, increase my faith" (see Luke 17:5), the will, desire, and motive to share the gospel will grow stronger and stronger.

Build Faith in God

The Prophet Joseph Smith referred to faith as "the moving cause of all action . . . without it both mind and body would be in a state of inactivity, and all [our] exertions would cease, both physical and mental" (see *Lectures on Faith* 1:7–12).

Orson F. Whitney adds: "Faith is the beating heart of the universe—the incentive, the impulse, to all action, the mainspring of all achievement. Nothing was ever accomplished, small or great, commonplace or miraculous, that was not backed up by confidence in some power, human or superhuman, that impelled and pushed forward the enterprise." (*Gospel Themes* [Salt Lake City: The Church of Jesus Christ of Latter-day Saints, 1914], p. 33.)

It is inconceivable that any missionary would enter the mission field without a belief in God. However, some do begin their service with tentative understandings and feelings, relying heavily upon the testimonies of parents and others. Therefore, mission presidents must say and do things that will change passive belief into active faith. Until a missionary knows his or her God well enough to declare "in [God's] strength I can do all things" (Alma 26:12), motivation will be limited.

The same can be said of all members, young or old. Unless passive belief is replaced by active faith in God, little or no effort will be made to share anything of worth.

A true believer expands his or her knowledge of God by searching the scriptures (see John 5:39), praying over all things (see Mosiah 5:13), reading the Book of Mormon (see 1 Nephi 6:1–6), bearing testimony (see Alma 6:8), talking of Christ (see 2 Nephi 25:26), and observing the evidences of Deity (see Alma 30:40–44). Impetus for these actions will come through the daily study of the scriptures, testimony meetings, and other gatherings of the Saints where they feel the presence of the Holy Spirit.

When a Church member possesses faith and believes there is a God in heaven, he or she has the strong desire to live in accord with divine will. He or she, therefore, keeps the commandments and tries to please Heavenly Father. In the process of doing so, the member is blessed and enabled to perform well beyond his or her natural abilities.

Belief in God leads to high standards and high expectations. High standards and expectations pull high performance from a person of integrity. Such transformation of belief to accelerated living and serving is an integral part of spiritual motivation.

Build Faith in One's Cause

Until a follower of Christ accepts God's purpose (see Moses 1:39) as his or her own personal cause, that person will have little enthusiasm for living or sharing the gospel! But when the disciple realizes that he or she has entered into a partnership with the Lord to assist in achieving the purpose of the eternal plan of salvation, zeal for the work increases and reaches new heights.

Leaders must help others understand the purposes of mortality (see Abraham 3:25), the plan of salvation (see Alma 42), the atonement of Jesus Christ (see 2 Nephi 2), the concept of agency (see 2 Nephi 10:23–25), and other aspects of the gospel. Otherwise, members fail to grasp the reason for their calls to service and the urgency of God's work. Leaders should also center special emphasis on the signs of the times and the fulfillment of prophecy.

Each missionary and member must understand that the gospel is rolling forth unto the ends of the earth (see D&C 65:1–6). We must not forget that Saints are "armed with righteousness and with the power of God in great glory" (1 Nephi 14:14). We must realize that the commission given to us is angelic in nature (see Moroni 7:29–31). We must believe that "the eternal purposes of the Lord shall roll on, until all his promises shall be fulfilled" (Mormon 8:22). We must "remember that it is not the work of God that is frustrated, but the work of men" (D&C 3:3).

The wise Church leader will take the time to review Church growth and to highlight the evidences of divine assistance. Such a review must not be to boast but to humbly acknowledge God's hand in accelerating the progress of the work. He will cite spiritual manifestations of divine power; he will encourage others to share spiritual experiences; and he will testify boldly concerning the future destiny of the Church.

Above all, the leader will emphasize to his associates the need to be "saviors of men" (see D&C 103:9–10) and to serve blamelessly before God (see D&C 4:2).

Build Faith in One's Leaders

Ernie Pyle, a World War II war correspondent, is reported to have said, "Nine-tenths of morale is made up of pride in your outfit and confidence in your leaders" (quoted in Sterling W. Sill, *The Strength of Great Possessions* [Salt Lake City: Bookcraft, 1970], p. 129). This statement seems to have special application to the person who is striving to be a "good soldier of Jesus Christ" (2 Timothy 2:3). As long as one feels that one's cause is just, that one's organization is right and proper, and that one's leader is a loving, caring, and inspired leader, one will strive to do one's part in keeping the system perfect and in building the Church (see D&C 84:109–110).

A motivating leader maintains a positive attitude, knowing that one who is downbeat and sour in demeanor can infect others with the dreaded disease. A wise leader knows that a negative state of mind, like a contagious virus, can run rampant through a group and disable many. On the other hand, a person with a positive point of view sends edifying verbal and nonverbal messages to others.

Therefore, the motivating leader reads the scriptures, prays always, engages in uplifting conversations, bears testimony, looks for the good in others, and counts blessings daily. He knows his followers, gives sincere praise and encouragement, and disciplines others in a loving, constructive, and uplifting manner. He is gentle but firm; he corrects with kindness but avoids causing embarrassment; he establishes personal relationships with others but does not play favorites; and he expects obedience but avoids the use of threats or ultimatums. When all of this is done, those who follow will say, "Our leaders were mighty men in the faith of the Lord; and they taught [us] the ways of the Lord; wherefore, we withstood [our enemies]" (Jarom 1:7).

I know of a military unit in which officers wore a special badge on their caps. Across the badge was a small sword and an inscription that read, "Take it and follow me." This badge reminded leaders that they were expected to set the right example before the troops. Each time I saw that badge, I was reminded of the divine invitation extended by the greatest Leader of all time, "Come, follow me" (Luke 18:22).

Many other things could be said about the imperative need of leaders to say and do those things that will cause followers to have faith in their leaders. It is my belief that a leader's challenge is to win the trust of his associates and help them gain a measure of success— real success.

It should be remembered that leadership is the process of persuasion and example—a process that transforms potential into reality. Therefore, a Church leader helps others discover the spiritual gifts within them, use the natural talents with which they are endowed, and release their motivational energies held in reserve. The leader's objective is to see that no follower is released, after his or her term of service, with any music unplayed or unsung. A person's music will be unplayed and unsung if he or she is not motivated to share with others the testimony and virtue that resides within him or her.

Concluding Words

In this chapter I have shared some thoughts about motivation. This has been done with two purposes in mind: to help members and missionaries understand what must occur in their minds and hearts if they desire to share the gospel with any degree of enthusiasm, and to help leaders understand what they must do to excite associates with the missionary spirit.

I have discussed four forms or levels of motivation: fear, reward, duty, and inner. I have also mentioned that professional motivators are using programs centered around gospel-rooted principles or approaches such as building self-image, fostering a positive mental attitude, encouraging goal-setting, and setting high standards and expectations.

Spiritual or inner motivation, I believe, is really *a matter of faith.* It develops when one builds faith in self, faith in God, faith in one's cause, and faith in one's leaders.

All members and leaders must come to the realization that the greatest force multiplier within the Church is the converted and motivated member. So long as only a few serve and share with all their "heart, might, mind and strength" (D&C 4:2), the productivity of the group is limited. But when all increase their faith and labor with "throbs in the heart," the power of the missionary force of the Church is multiplied many, many times over.

The central issue of the Church's missionary program is and always will be the willingness of the Saints to live the gospel of Jesus Christ and to serve their fellowmen. There is no substitute for faithful and devoted members and missionaries who believe in themselves, their God, and their cause and who are led by leaders who know what they are doing. These are the spur and reins whereby all are set to work and guided in saving souls.

7

MERITS

A Treasure Chest of Blessings

Wherefore, seek not the things of this world but seek ye first to build up the kingdom of God, and to establish his righteousness; and all these things shall be added unto you (Joseph Smith Translation, Matthew 6:38; cf. King James Version, Matthew 6:33).

The seventh M of missionary service is merits—referring to that veritable endless flow of blessings that comes to those who "remain steadfast . . . in bearing testimony to all the world" (D&C 84:61).

Introduction

Many years ago I delayed my formal education, gave up a promising sports career, and interrupted my marriage to serve a full-time mission for the Church. At the time I felt that I was making a significant personal sacrifice and placing my all upon the altar of God. Some well-meaning people added to my feelings of self-pity by saying I was giving away my future; others said I was forfeiting the best years of my life. Yes, I was led to presume that by serving the mission, I would place the Lord deeply in my debt.

How very wrong I was! Even before my mission ended, the blessings came flowing upon me. And that stream of goodness from heaven has continued over the years and seems to be never-ending. What little I gave to the Lord has been returned to me in "good measure, pressed down, and shaken together, and running over" (Luke

6:38). No, the mission was not a sacrifice; it was a simple test of my faith and a time for God to verify his promise: "Seek not the things of this world, but seek ye first to build up the kingdom of God, and to establish his righteousness; and all these things shall be added unto you" (Joseph Smith Translation, Matthew 6:38; cf. King James Version, Matthew 6:33).

The test of my faith and the verification of God's promise did not end with my release as a full-time missionary. It was only the beginning!

Nearly fifty years have come and gone since my return from the Palestine-Syrian or Near Eastern Mission. Over and over again I have been tempted to chase after the things of the world and to forsake efforts to help build up the Church. But each time the temptation has presented itself in its various forms, my love of God and testimony of the restored gospel have prevailed and held me on course. Such love and testimony have been nurtured by my activity in the wards and stakes in which I have lived, particularly that activity associated with missionary service.

If my service as a full-time missionary was measured solely by the number of convert baptisms performed, I would have been declared a failure because very few people joined the Church as a result of my proselyting efforts. My success as a member-missionary, however, is another story. I have been privileged to play a small part in the conversion of a number of people while serving as a bishop, quorum leader, and high councilor. With each conversion, "all these things" have been added, verifying the promise that the merits of missionary service are never-ending, whether performed by full-time missionaries or member missionaries.

What Is a Merit?

The word *merit* is defined as "reward . . . : just deserts" (*Webster's Third New International Dictionary*). Such a definition often turns our minds to temporal gains received for service rendered. It also suggests a dollar return on a dollar invested and nothing more.

Another definition, however, refers to *merit* as "spiritual credit or stored moral surplusage regarded as earned by performance of righteous acts and as ensuring future benefits" (ibid.). This latter definition appeals to me and seems to apply to missionary service because the process of sharing the gospel with others is centered in "righteous acts" and carries "future benefits" for both the giver and the receiver. In fact, the list of spiritual credits or by-products received by those who seek to save souls is endless. Those who engage in missionary service soon learn that God is a very generous paymaster. We can never place him in our debt (see Mosiah 2:22–24).

What's in It for Me?

A host of merits is promised to those who publish peace in all the world; just ask any missionary or disciple of Christ who has done so with clean hands and a pure heart. But before we list these spiritual credits and moral surpluses, it is important that we say a few words about the sincere desires that must accompany missionary service if the merits are to be claimed.

When you have been invited to do something, have you ever thought to yourself, *What's in it for me?* Such a response is not uncommon among people of the world who have been conditioned to expect a return on investments of time, money, or energy. *After all,* you say to yourself, *my time is precious and so are my resources.*

Perhaps the "what's in it for me" attitude diminishes as we push aside worldly desires and elect to participate in religious affairs. This ought to be the case, because we engage in such activities voluntarily. Moreover, things of the Spirit do tend to direct minds away from self and more toward others, especially those who are crying out for help. Still, the natural man within most of us makes it difficult for us to give alms in secret without the left hand knowing what the right hand is doing (see Matthew 6:3–4). Only the exceptional few, it seems, put their hands to the plow and move forward without reaching back to grab a reward for efforts expended (see Luke 9:62).

Jesus' invitations to his disciples were simply stated and free of any carrot dangling on the end of a stick. His entreaty was, "Come, follow me" (Luke 18:22) or "Come and see" (John 1:39). He did not offer his followers a salary, an expense account, or other worldly incentives. All that he offered his fellow servants were the things that money cannot buy—things referred to as the riches of eternity.

We meet occasionally a person of deep faith who obeys commandments and sacrifices his or her time and means in behalf of Godly purposes as willingly as did Adam. Adam was asked by an angel why he offered sacrifices unto the Lord. He responded, "I know not, save the Lord commanded me" (Moses 5:6). A recital of promised blessings related to sacrificial offerings was not required in his case. Moreover, he didn't wait with hands in pockets until someone delivered him a doctrinal discourse on the symbolism and merits of sacrifice. He obeyed because he believed, and that was the conclusion of the matter.

Unfortunately, not all of us possess the purity of motive or depth of faith that propels us to obey God independent of promised blessings. We like to know all about the promises proffered those who live the Word of Wisdom. We like to hear about the windows of heaven and the blessings that will be poured out upon us if we pay our tithing. Yes, it seems that the "what's in it for me" attitude is one of the more difficult parts of the natural man that we are challenged to put off or overcome (see Mosiah 3:19).

As stated before, the "what's in it for me" attitude usually becomes more and more subliminal as the person sharing the gospel gains spiritual maturity, becomes acquainted with pure motive, loses himself or herself in charitable acts, and catches the spirit of missionary service. Let me share a personal experience to illustrate this point.

Do You Recognize This Man?

Early one morning I received a telephone call from a distraught missionary who insisted upon an immediate interview. I obliged the young man because I feared that something might be awry in his life.

He initiated the conversation by showing me a picture of a long-haired, hippie-type person and asking, "Do you recognize the man in the picture?" I said that I didn't and wondered what kind of a game he was playing with me.

After some delay and an awkward moment or two, he confessed: "That is a picture of me taken only a few weeks before I received my mission call. You see, there was a time when I lived a rather reckless life and cared little about church and religion. When I learned that I might win the love of my girlfriend and please my angel mother by serving a mission, I cleaned up my life and made myself available for service."

The missionary explained to me that he had determined that he could endure any experience—even a two-year mission—if it would please the two most important women in his life. "But," the young man confided, "I did not count on one thing. I didn't count on getting converted." With some emotion, he admitted that his motive for serving was wrong and that he was ashamed of himself.

I commended the missionary for his honesty and assured him that he was not the first, nor would he be the last, to go through such a conversion process. I promised him that his work would become more significant and his efforts more productive now that his motives for serving had been purged. I pointed out that even greater blessings or merits would be his if he served with all of his heart, might, mind, and strength.

What Is the Principle of Serendipity?

The experience with the young man who began his missionary odyssey with the hope of gaining the love of his girlfriend and mother and who discovered something valuable in the process brings to mind a Persian fairy tale called *The Three Princes of Serendip*. These three men began a special adventure similar to the quests conducted by medieval knights. While striving to reach their destination and to complete their difficult task, they found many valuable gifts not sought for along the way. Thus the word *serendipity* came to mean any discovery of gifts, treasures, merits, or blessings not sought for in the process of performing a worthy service or seeking something else.

Incidentally, the king and father of the three princes sent them on their quest trusting that they would acquire three things: virtue, science, and wisdom. He must have known something about the principle of serendipity, and he was certainly acquainted with the things that matter most.

What Are the Merits of Missionary Service?

Many will attest that the principle of serendipity applies to missionary service more than perhaps any other work, for it is a truly meritorious service. Among the more significant merits of sharing the gospel are the following:

Feeling Deep and Abiding Joy

An oft-quoted scripture reads: "Remember the worth of souls is great in the sight of God. . . . And how great is his joy in the soul that repenteth! . . . And if it so be that you should labor all your days in crying repentance unto this people, and bring, save it be one soul unto me, how great shall be your joy with him in the kingdom of my Father!" (D&C 18:10, 13, 15.)

Joy in this context is not a fleeting feeling or a passing pleasure; it is deep and abiding happiness. President Heber J. Grant testified: "[I] had more joy while in the mission field than ever before or since. Man is that he may have joy, and the joy that I had in the mission field was superior to any I have ever experienced elsewhere." ("The President Speaks," *Improvement Era*, November 1936, p. 659.) This is a statement made by a man who had traveled worldwide and who had participated in almost every phase of gospel activity.

Others have said the same about stake missionary and member-missionary service. Converts are the "glory and joy" (1 Thessalonians 2:20) of all who proclaim the gospel irrespective of where they live or what their church assignment may be at the moment.

Our hearts are touched by the account of Ammon's and Alma's joy as they met with missionary associates who "had waxed strong in the knowledge of the truth" (Alma 17:2). Among other things, Ammon said: "My joy is full, yea, my heart is brim with joy, and I will rejoice in my God. . . . I cannot say the smallest part which I feel." (Alma 26:11, 16.) Joy—deep and abiding joy—is unquestionably the crown-jewel merit of missionary service.

Obtaining a Peace of Conscience

Peace of conscience, I believe, is synonymous with peace of mind. It is a quiet, calm feeling that comes to a person who has done the right thing at the right time for the right reason.

Most of us know that living prophets have made appeals for a more missionary-minded people. This fact has become registered in our minds and hearts. We know that the need to proclaim the gospel is real. We believe in the prophets who have issued the call. Therefore, full peace of conscience will not come until we have obeyed the command, heeded the prophets' call, and served!

Elder George Albert Smith taught: "It is not an easy task; it is not a pleasant thing, perhaps, to be called out into the world, to leave our dear ones, but I say to you that it will purchase for those who are faithful, for those who discharge that obligation as they may be required, *peace and happiness beyond all understanding,* and will prepare them that, in due time, when life's labor is complete, they will stand in the presence of their Maker, accepted of Him because of what they have done" (in Conference Report, April 1922, p. 53; emphasis added).

The same holds true for those who serve at home and never leave their communities. It isn't always easy to approach our neighbor and extend the hand of friendship to someone who doesn't believe and love as we do.

Increasing One's Knowledge of the Gospel

Full-time missionaries are asked to study the gospel and related subjects at least two hours every day. One hour is generally designated for individual study, and the other hour is for study with one's companion. If my calculations are correct, a twenty-four-month mission provides a missionary with the opportunity of studying the gospel of Jesus Christ and the missionary discussions a minimum of 1,460 hours or the equivalent of sixty-one days.

By simply following the approved missionary gospel study plan, a missionary will read the Book of Mormon, the New Testament, the Doctrine and Covenants, and parts of the Old Testament several times. Additionally, he or she will study basic gospel topics in depth as he or she masters the missionary discussions.

Some missionaries teach an average of twenty discussions or more per week. This amounts to 1,500 to 2,000 discussions during their term of service. Just think of the truths the missionary internalizes as he or she teaches these lessons over and over again and responds to questions along the way. I remind you that one really never clinches one's learning until one has taught. Missions are indeed schools for future prophets.

The need to search the scriptures and increase one's knowledge of the gospel is not the exclusive right of full-time missionaries. It is an ongoing responsibility of all Church members. I'm convinced that one's desire and willingness to share the gospel waxes stronger and stronger as new insights and truths are acquired by stake and full-time missionaries and member-missionaries.

Making a Leap in Faith

Elder James E. Talmage describes belief as passive acceptance of truth. Faith, however, he defines as active acceptance of truth that leads to good works. (See *The Articles of Faith*, 12th ed. [Salt Lake City: The Church of Jesus Christ of Latter-day Saints, 1924], pp. 96–97.) Some begin their missionary service simply because they believe. They believe that Jesus is the Christ, that the restored gospel is true, and that they should serve. During their service, as they pray for contacts, plead for help in teaching, and struggle for the right words, a leap from passive belief to active faith occurs.

Full-time missionaries and member-missionaries not only see but participate frequently in miraculous healings. They see people forsake sin and become Saints. They receive answers to prayers, feel the promptings of the Spirit, and observe the gift of tongues and many other operations of the Spirit. They also feel that unseen powers are sustaining them. These and many other experiences plant seeds of faith in their hearts. In fact, some missionaries nourish the seed of faith so well with the word of God that it becomes almost perfect during their terms of service (see Alma 32).

Drawing Nearer to the Lord

President Heber J. Grant said: "Get it into your hearts . . . to prepare yourselves to go out into the world where you can get on your knees and draw nearer to the Lord than in any other labor" ("The President Speaks," *Improvement Era*, November 1936, p. 659).

If you serve and become an instrument in the hands of the Lord, you will come to know him and to love him. You will draw nearer to the source of your power, even Jesus the Christ.

Ask any stake or full-time missionary, "What was the greatest thing about your mission?" Usually the answer is, "It gave me an opportunity to draw closer to the Lord."

Courting the Companionship of the Holy Spirit

I love the words of Elder Thomas S. Monson: "When we share the gospel with others, we unavoidably get outside of ourselves: we think and pray and work for the blessing of others, and this only further enriches and quickens us by the Holy Spirit" ("Status Report on Missionary Work," *Ensign*, October 1977, p. 11).

What Spirit pervades this work? It is the Holy Ghost. For he is the testifier; he is the converter. The Pauls may plant; the Apolloses may water; but God, through the Holy Ghost, always gives the increase (see 1 Corinthians 3:6).

Of all the companionships established during missionary service, the most cherished is the companionship of the Holy Spirit. We learn to recognize his voice; we tend to heed his warnings; and we feel his closeness while bearing testimony and seeking to lift others. Do become acquainted with this member of the Godhead and court his influence all the remainder of your days.

Strengthening One's Testimony

A testimony is much like a muscle. It grows when it is used. It atrophies when unused. Initially it may be small and weak. But as it is exercised it is strengthened.

Missionaries teach and testify, teach and testify, teach and testify. Each time they do, they invite the Spirit and the truths they proclaim become more and more deeply ingrained in their own souls. The witness voiced by eternal truths becomes brighter and clearer and more effective with each testimony given.

Brigham Young promised: "Those faithful Elders who have testified of this work to thousands of people on the continents and islands of the seas will see the fruits of their labors, whether they have said five words or thousands. They may not see these fruits immediately, and perhaps, in many cases, not until the Millennium; *but the savor of their testimony* will pass down from father to son." (*Discourses of Brigham Young*, sel. John A. Widtsoe [Salt Lake City: Deseret Book Co., 1978], p. 329; emphasis added.) Cannot the same be said of lay members of the Church who testify to friends close at home?

Receiving a Forgiveness of Sins

President Spencer W. Kimball stated: "The Lord has told us that our sins will be forgiven more readily as we bring souls unto Christ and remain steadfast in bearing testimony to the world, and surely every one of us is looking for additional help in being forgiven of our sins" ("'It Becometh Every Man,'" *Ensign*, October 1977, p. 3).

I'll never forget an experience I had in Australia a few years ago. My wife and I had been invited to participate in a mission confer-ence. As a part of that conference program, some missionaries sang and testified. One of the participants was a young man who had a spe-cial glow upon his face. In fact, my wife observed, "I've never seen anyone sparkle with the truth as he does."

When the meeting finished, before I could even leave the stand this young man said, "Elder Asay, may I speak with you?"

I turned to the mission president and said, "Do you mind if I speak with this young man?"

He said, "Oh no, be my guest."

I said to the young man: "Go down to the bishop's office and wait; I'll be there shortly." He turned and walked down the aisle.

When he was out of earshot, I turned back to the mission presi-dent and asked, "Do you suppose there's a problem here?"

His response was, "Couldn't be. He's a living legend already in this mission."

At the bishop's office, the missionary was so conscious of my time that he wouldn't even let me sit down. He said, "Elder Asay, you have forgotten me, haven't you?"

"Yes, I guess I have," I admitted. "Please forgive me."

Then he said, "Several years ago I came to your office with my bishop and stake president. I came because I had done many foolish things in high school, I had made myself unworthy of my priesthood, and I required some special clearance before I could serve. In fact, you may recall that when I gave you a listing of my transgressions, you said, 'I will never allow you to serve.'"

Then I remembered. I remembered that his sins were so reprehen-sible to me that I said, "No, you can't serve!" He pled, his bishop pled, and his stake president pled for special consideration. Finally I re-lented by saying, "You may serve on two conditions: first, that you live every commandment strictly; and second, that you will seek to become the best missionary in your assigned mission."

He said, "Elder Asay, it thrilled me to know that you were coming to this mission. Next week I go home, and I just wanted to report that for two years now I haven't stretched or bent or broken a single rule or commandment."

"God bless you for that," I responded.

And then he added, "I may not be the best missionary in this mission, but I'm awfully close."

I thanked him for his wonderful report. He walked to the door, turned back, and added, "Elder Asay, for the first time in many, many years I feel perfectly clean."

I said, "You are. You have been sanctified by your service. Now, please go home and don't lose what you have gained."

One of our modern Apostles, George F. Richards, promised: "In the name of the Lord I want to promise you that in the acceptance of the mission call and the dedication of yourself to the work, the Lord will forgive you of past transgressions, and you can start out life with an absolutely clean sheet." Who wouldn't want to claim that merit?

Developing and Polishing Character

Stephen L Richards, in a memorable conference address, talked about the influence of missions upon the Latter-day Saints. He listed all of the by-products of missionary service and stated, "Such benefits, however, while important, are but incidental. The more vital results are deeper than enlarged information and polish. The fundamental character of our manhood and womanhood has been improved. Sacrifice has taught self-control. Giving has made for generosity as it always does. Teaching the virtues has brought them into application, and high spirituality has ingrained testimony and soul development." (In Conference Report, October 1945, p. 55.)

If my understanding of character is right, it is in part made up of habits and inclinations that we have developed over the years. Just think of the habits, the tendencies, the inclinations, the virtues that can be acquired through missionary service. I name only a few: daily gospel study, daily prayer, daily planning, good grooming, early rising, love for people, strict obedience to rules, hard work, compatible living with companions, memorization of truths, and the list goes on.

Who has not seen the reflection of sterling qualities in the faces of members and missionaries who have mastered such habits? Who has not observed firsthand the development and polishing of character that occurs in such a few short months of service?

Becoming a Peacemaker

The Savior has said, "Blessed are the peacemakers: for they shall be called the children of God" (Matthew 5:9). Elder N. Eldon Tanner spoke these words: "If every member of this Church would accept the call of our prophet today and live the gospel and keep the commandments of our Heavenly Father and become missionaries in very deed, we could contribute *more to the cause of peace* than all the power that might be gathered together by all the governments and all the men in uniform" (in Conference Report, October 1962, p. 69; emphasis added).

Our privilege is to share the gospel of peace! In other words, to become a contributing member of God's peace corps. I don't fault the U.S. Peace Corps that was established in 1961. Much good has been derived through this government effort. Still, the greatest peace movement and the greatest peace corps is the one that involves members and full-time missionaries who represent the Prince of Peace.

Developing a Love and Understanding of People

Few people love the Armenian people more than I do. Why? Because I served among them. I learned to speak some of their language. I have studied their history. I have become acquainted with their customs and culture. And I have tried to add to their rich religious tradition. I love them with all of my heart.

One returned missionary, now a physician, who interrupted his academic studies to serve a mission, expressed: "Full-time missionary work brought about an increased love and concern for others. 'Intelligence alone is not enough. . . . Intelligence plus a Christlike love for mankind is the perfect combination for a successful and respected physician.'" (Quoted in Rosemary Peck, "Time Out for a Mission," *New Era*, June 1980, p. 9.)

Establishing Abiding Friendships

Virtually every full-time missionary has the privilege of living and laboring with at least five or six companions. In the course of eating and praying and teaching together, they develop special bonds of friendship. Some of those friendships are of the David and Jonathan variety, and they persist throughout life. The bonds of friendship established in the mission field never are broken. They seem to be of the eternal type. I know the missionaries that I served with so many years ago are almost like brothers to me. We are kindred spirits and soul brothers in the finest sense. And why not? We did the work of the Lord side by side.

Think also of all the lifetime friendships that missionaries establish with people they teach and baptize. No one loves a missionary quite like a convert. Ask any convert, "Can you name the missionary or member who exposed you to the gospel?" The answer will be, "Oh yes, yes!" And then if you ask, "How do you feel about those who brought you the truth?" a tear will surface and the convert will say, "They are the greatest! They were saviors to me!"

Experiencing High Adventure

President Kimball has referred to missionary service as high adventure. He did so because the work is stirring and exciting. It is a bold undertaking, and it is one that requires the finest courage. I don't care if one serves in south Salt Lake or southern France or southern Brazil or southern Thailand. Each place has its own adventure to give.

I once saw a movie advertisement that read, "Greatest adventure story of escape." I thought to myself, *They don't know what adventure is until they have tried to help someone escape from sin, or have pulled somebody back from the brink of a spiritual death, or have wrestled with evil forces, or have marched with the army of God.* No greater adventure, no more excitement, nothing is more stirring than service in the work of the Lord.

Developing Language and Verbal Skills

Full-time missionaries are laboring in many sovereign countries, territories, colonies, or possessions. Missions extend from Utah to Australia, India, and other faraway places with strange-sounding names.

Language training at the Missionary Training Center and the infield training that follows can net a returned missionary as much as sixteen semester hours or twenty-four quarter hours of university credit, providing he takes the proper classes and passes the proficiency tests.

Imagine the language skills a person develops who reads and speaks and writes as extensively as do missionaries. Francis Bacon said: "Reading makes a full man; conversation a ready man; and writing an exact man." There is no greater development and no better place to cultivate language skills than in missionary service performed at home or abroad.

Preparing for Christ's Second Coming

How very privileged we are to be a part of fulfillment of prophecy! What an honor to be invited to build the kingdom, to serve in an Elias role in preparation for the second coming of the Savior. No work is more urgent, no work is more important than building and preparing for Christ's coming.

The story is told of a student athlete who turned down lucrative scholarship offers from several universities to serve a mission. Some relatives and friends were appalled by his decision and told him that he was wasting his future. He could not be dissuaded. Among other things, he said in response to the sharp criticism leveled against him: "I know that Christ will come again. And when he does come, I don't want to be found in some swimming pool practicing the breaststroke."

Developing Leadership Traits and Skills

On one occasion I participated in a stake reorganization in Colombia. I interviewed some men, hoping that the Lord would reveal to me the new stake president. The man called was a returned missionary of less than thirty years of age. Although short in years, he was long in spirit and experience. He had served a mission. He had been a mission leader. He was prepared to serve and to lead. In answer to my question, "How can I help you?" he simply replied, "Teach me."

Missionaries, stake and full-time, are extended many positions of trust. Each assignment, if fulfilled properly, will groom one for callings in the wards and stakes of the Church. Missionary service is in many respects a leadership-training program.

Yes, returned missionaries do indeed constitute the backbone of the Church.

Rendering Service to God and Man

Elder Thomas S. Monson said: "The eternal truth is: that which we willingly share, we keep; and that which we selfishly keep to ourselves, we lose" ("Status Report on Missionary Work," *Ensign*, October 1977, p. 11). It is as simple as that.

You are familiar with the inspired teachings of King Benjamin. Among other things, he said: "When ye are in the service of your fellow beings ye are only in the service of your God. . . . If ye should serve him with all your whole souls yet ye would be unprofitable servants. . . . He hath created you, and granted unto you your lives, for which ye are indebted unto him. And secondly, he doth require that ye should do as he hath commanded you; for which if ye do, he doth immediately bless you; and therefore he hath paid you. And ye are still indebted unto him, and are, and will be, forever and ever; therefore, of what have ye to boast?" (Mosiah 2:17, 21, 23–24.)

Learning to Sacrifice

Sacrifice has been referred to as the crowning test of the gospel. Joseph Smith taught, "A religion that does not require the sacrifice of all things never has power sufficient to produce the faith necessary [to lead] unto life and salvation" (*Lectures on Faith* 6:7).

In response to the rich young man's query about how to obtain eternal life, the Savior answered that he must be willing to sacrifice all that he had for the Lord and his cause. Said Jesus, "If thou wilt be perfect, go and sell that thou hast, and give to the poor, and thou shalt have treasure in heaven: and come and follow me." (See Matthew 19:16–29; D&C 132:55.)

How does the principle and practice of sacrifice apply in a modern world? What sacrifices are we required to make in the twentieth century? What do we place upon God's altar?

President Spencer W. Kimball stated: "We must lay on the altar and sacrifice whatever is required by the Lord. We begin by offering a 'broken heart and a contrite spirit.' We follow this by giving our best effort in our assigned fields of labor and callings. Finally we consecrate our time, talents, and means as called upon by our file leaders and as prompted by the whisperings of the Spirit. . . . And as we give, we find that 'sacrifice brings forth the blessings of heaven!' (*Hymns*, no. 147.) And in the end, we learn it was no sacrifice at all." (In Conference Report, April 1978, pp. 123–24.)

God help us all to climb our personal mountains of Moriah and place our all upon the altar of God. In so doing, we shall be blessed beyond measure and demonstrate our devotion to a loving Father in Heaven and his Son, the "great and last sacrifice" (Alma 34:14), in whose debt we shall stand eternally. (See Carlos E. Asay, *In the Lord's Service* [Salt Lake City: Deseret Book Co., 1990], pp. 162–63.)

Obtaining Eternal Life

The greatest gift of all of the gifts given by God is eternal life. I love the words of George Albert Smith: "We spend most of our time, many of us, seeking the things of this life that we will be compelled to leave when we go from here, yet there are the immortal souls all around us whom, if we would, we could teach and inspire to investigate the truth, and implant in their hearts a knowledge that God lives. What treasure in all the world could be so precious to us, for we would have their gratitude here and their everlasting and eternal appreciation in the world to come." (In Conference Report, October 1916, p. 50.)

Moreover, as I understand it, those who serve and help save become candidates for eternal life. It should be remembered that our salvation is intertwined with the salvation of others, and only by reaching down and lifting up can we hope to move ourselves heavenward. Furthermore, only one road leads to eternal life; we can stay on that path best by helping others find it and walk it.

Fix your mind on this promise of the Master: "And every one that hath forsaken houses, or brethren, or sisters, or father, or mother, or wife, or children, or lands, for my name's sake, shall receive an hundredfold, and shall *inherit everlasting life*" (Matthew 19:29; emphasis added).

Conclusion

I have cited nineteen merits pertaining to missionary service. There are more, many more. The treasure chest is full to overflowing. Please understand that these blessings can be yours, if you serve the Lord properly.

Elder David O. McKay taught:

Many of us fail to realize the value and potent possibilities of this great branch of Church activity [missionary work].
1. As an example of voluntary service in the cause of the Master, it is unexcelled.
2. As an incentive to clean living among youth, as a contributing factor to character building, its influence is immeasurable.
3. As an educative force and uplifting influence upon our communities, its effect is clearly manifest.
4. As a contributing factor to a better understanding among nations, and to the establishing of international friendship, it wields a significant influence.
5. As it is the purpose of the Almighty to save the individual, not to make him a mere cog in the machinery of the state, the missionary service works most harmoniously in the consummation of this eternal plan! (In Conference Report, October 1949, p. 117.)

Said President Kimball, "Missionary work, like the tithing, will pour out blessings, as Malachi said, so many blessings that there'll hardly be room enough to receive them" (in Korea Area Conference Report, August 1975, p. 61). I believe that. Almost every conceivable spiritual blessing is in some way related to full-time missionary service. It is a service overflowing with merits because the principle of serendipity is its fountainhead.

A number of years ago, while laboring in the Palestine-Syrian Mission, I was set apart for a calling by President Alma Sonne of the European Mission. At the conclusion of the blessing, I thanked Elder Sonne for the beautiful and inspiring words he had spoken. He graciously accepted my expression of gratitude; however, he placed his hand upon my shoulder, looked intently into my eyes, and said, "Elder Asay, I had the power and right to say what I said, but remember, you will write your own blessing by the way you live and serve." Then he added, "Go and write the best blessing that has ever been written."

Over the years Elder Sonne's words, "You will write your own blessing by the way you live and serve," have echoed again and again in my mind.

Whether you are called to perform missionary services at home or abroad, I challenge you as Elder Sonne challenged me to abide by the laws, expectations, and conditions linked to your calling and to go and write the best blessing that has ever been written.

One of our hymns contains the invitation, "Do what is right. . . . Blessings await you." ("Do What Is Right," in *Hymns*, no. 237.) Such is the invitation and promise of missionary service.

Would you like your testimony recorded in heaven? Would you like angels to rejoice over you? Would you like to receive a forgiveness of sins? Would you like to receive the nineteen merits mentioned? If you do, remember that all of these blessings are promised those who "remain steadfast in [their] minds in solemnity and the spirit of prayer, in bearing testimony to all the world" (D&C 84:61).

Whoever destroys a single life is as guilty as though he had destroyed the entire world; and whoever rescues a single life earns as much merit as though he had rescued the entire world (Talmud, Mishna, Sanhedrin).

"How Beautiful Upon the Mountains Are the Feet of Him That Bringeth Good Tidings"

The Lighter Side

Sometime ago I mentioned to a friend of mine that I was scheduled to speak to a group of people and that my subject was "How Beautiful Are Their Feet." "Oh," he responded, "are you speaking at a convention of podiatrists?" I don't suppose that many beyond the postal service, mountaineers, or the infantry regard the feet as objects of beauty, except, of course, the Saints who have searched the scriptures and gained an appreciation for missionaries and missionary service.

I am not a connoisseur of feet, and I never have been. In fact, I have never felt that something usually sweaty and smelly and covered with corns, bunions, warts, callouses, ingrown toenails, and hammer-toes was very attractive. But I was interested in learning that my two feet—size 10 1/2 D—include 50 bones and 76 joints, with muscles, ligaments, and nerves, all working in a synchronized way to provide me needed support, balance, and motion.

I was also interested in learning that foot pain can be a symptom of serious problems—like diabetes, heart disease, kidney disorders, or arthritis. The Apostle Paul must have known all of this about feet when he wrote: "And the eye cannot say unto the hand, I have no

need of thee: nor again the head to the feet, I have no need of you"
(1 Corinthians 12:21). All members or parts of the body of Christ are
necessary and important. The feet, however, seem to occupy a special
place in holy writ—a space worthy of our serious thought.

"What Meaneth the Words?"

Some 148 years B.C., one of King Noah's wicked priests asked the
prophet Abinadi:

> What meaneth the words which are written, and which have
> been taught by our fathers, saying:
> How beautiful upon the mountains are the feet of him that
> bringeth good tidings; that publisheth peace; that bringeth good tid-
> ings of good; that publisheth salvation; that saith unto Zion, Thy
> God reigneth;
> Thy watchmen shall lift up the voice; with the voice together
> shall they sing; for they shall see eye to eye when the Lord shall bring
> again Zion;
> Break forth into joy; sing together ye waste places of Jerusalem;
> for the Lord hath comforted his people, he hath redeemed Jerusalem;
> The Lord hath made bare his holy arm in the eyes of all the na-
> tions, and all the ends of the earth shall see the salvation of our God?
> (Mosiah 12:20–24; see also Isaiah 52:7–9.)

Noah's apostate priests had read the words of Isaiah but had not
inquired of the Lord or searched for the proper meaning of the words
handed down by their fathers. Like others who had failed to give
"heed and diligence" to the word of God, the "mysteries of God" had
been withheld from them (see Alma 12:9–10). Therefore, Abinadi
had reason to answer them in a condemning manner: "Are you
priests, and pretend to teach this people, and to understand the spirit
of prophesying, and yet desire to know of me what these things mean?
I say unto you, wo be unto you for perverting the ways of the Lord!
For if ye understand these things ye have not taught them; therefore,
ye have perverted the ways of the Lord. Ye have not applied your
hearts to understanding; therefore, ye have not been wise. Therefore,
what teach ye this people?" (Mosiah 12:25–27.)

Three Applications

Later on in the Book of Mormon record, Abinadi asks his accusers two questions relating to Christ and the words of Isaiah: "Who shall declare his generation?" and "Who shall be his seed?" (Mosiah 15:10.) Abinadi then identifies three groups as those with beautiful feet who would become Christ's seed and heirs of the kingdom of God.

"They Who Have Published Peace"

One group was addressed as "they *who have* published peace, *who have* brought good tidings of good, *who have* published salvation; and said unto Zion: Thy God reigneth! And O how beautiful upon the mountains *were* their feet!" (Mosiah 15:14–15; emphasis added.) This category of prophets and Saints includes all of those who have performed missionary service, such as Christ's Apostles, the sons of Mosiah, Alma, and others. Even Ammon, Aaron, Omner, and Himni had beautiful feet despite their long and arduous walkabout among the Lamanites for fourteen years. It was said of them: "And thus they were instruments in the hands of God in bringing many to the knowledge of the truth, yea, to the knowledge of their Redeemer. And how blessed are they! For they did publish peace; they did publish good tidings of good; and they did declare unto the people that the Lord reigneth." (Mosiah 27:36–37.)

No one is more beautiful or more blessed than those who serve God by preaching and exemplifying the truth. It is the most sanctifying and beautifying labor of all!

Alma and those who assisted him at the Waters of Mormon were saviors of men, and they had beautiful feet. Note this beautiful tribute paid to Alma and his associates: "How beautiful are they to the eyes of them who there came to the knowledge of their Redeemer; yea, and how blessed are they, for they shall sing to his praise forever" (Mosiah 18:30).

"Those That Are Still Publishing Peace"

A second group mentioned by Abinadi are the missionaries of the present: "And again, how beautiful upon the mountains *are* the feet of those that *are still* publishing peace!" (Mosiah 15:16; emphasis added.)

I like what Paul had to say about preachers or missionaries. He instructed the Romans: "For whosoever shall call upon the name of the Lord shall be saved. How then shall they call on him in whom they have not believed? and how shall they believe in him of whom they have not heard? and how shall they hear without a preacher? And how shall they preach, except they be sent? as it is written, How beautiful are the feet of them that preach the gospel of peace, and bring glad tidings of good things!" (Romans 10:13–15.)

The feet, the voices, the faces, and the whole being of those preachers who share saving truths will always be precious and beautiful to new converts, especially to those who have suffered in their sins. In the eyes of those who have learned of Christ and of his power to save, there are few if any blemishes in the missionaries who walked long distances to bring the gospel message.

"Those Who Shall Hereafter Publish Peace"

The third group referenced by Abinadi is described as follows: "And again, how beautiful upon the mountains are the feet of those who shall hereafter publish peace, yea, from this time henceforth and forever!" (Mosiah 15:17; emphasis added.)

At a time when most missionaries came from the intermountain part of the United States, Orson Hyde declared: "And 'how beautiful upon the mountains are the feet of him that publisheth peace, and bringeth glad tidings to the meek.' That is, in other words, how beautiful are the feet of them that come from the mountains, bringing glad tidings unto the meek. How enviable is their position. There are no beings upon earth that, in reality, are so dignified and exalted as the men that have these glad tidings to proclaim to the world, though the world may not know it—may not see them in their true character." (In *Journal of Discourses* 6:31.)

Now that missionaries of today are being called from nations worldwide, it might be said: How beautiful upon the mountains, plains, hills, coasts, and valleys are the feet of all who publish peace. Missionaries and Saints of the past, present, and future, irrespective of where they come from or where they preach, will always be regarded as beautiful, head to foot, by those who have been blessed by their efforts to share the gospel of Jesus Christ. Moreover, if they remain faithful and steadfast in their living and preaching, the promise is that they will become the seed of Christ and heirs of the kingdom of God.

Christ's Beautiful Feet

Abinadi concludes his sermon about publishers of peace by saying: "And behold, I say unto you, this is not all. For O how beautiful upon the mountains are the feet of him that bringeth good tidings, that is the founder of peace, yea, even the Lord, who has redeemed his people; yea, him who has granted salvation unto his people." (Mosiah 15:18.)

No feet were, are, or ever will be more beautiful than the feet of our Lord and Savior Jesus Christ. I speak of the feet belonging to the Prince of Peace who walked the dusty roads of Judea so many years ago preaching and performing miracles. I refer to the feet of that Sinless One who permitted false accusers to pierce his hands and feet with iron nails that held him on the cross. I think of those beautiful feet of the one who stood in the air above Joseph Smith in the Sacred Grove and upon invitation of his Father announced the opening of the dispensation of the fulness of times.

How can any of us forget that solemn occasion when Jesus took a towel, girded himself, poured water into a basin, and washed the feet of his disciples. You will recall that Peter hesitated, saying, "Thou shalt never wash my feet." Jesus answered, "If I wash thee not, thou hast no part with me." To which Peter quickly responded, "Lord, not my feet only, but also my hands and my head." (See John 13:8–10.)

The significance of Christ washing the feet of his disciples is beyond the understanding of most people. Inasmuch as this recorded incident introduces a sacred gospel ordinance, an in-depth discussion of its symbolism is reserved for another time and place (see Bruce R. McConkie, *Doctrinal New Testament Commentary*, 3 vols. [Salt Lake City: Bookcraft, 1965–1973], 1:707–711).

However, all of us, even the gospel novice, can appreciate Peter's desires to place everything on the altar of God, including his hands, head, and feet. Should we not do the same and do all within our power to become heralds of righteousness with beautiful feet?

Concluding Word

Nearly 600 years B.C., the prophet Nephi saw in vision the restoration of the gospel in the latter days and the building up of Zion. Included with his glorious views of the future was this assurance: "And blessed are they who shall seek to bring forth my Zion at that day, for they shall have the gift and the power of the Holy Ghost; and if they endure unto the end they shall be lifted up at the last day, and shall be saved in the everlasting kingdom of the Lamb; and whoso shall pub-lish peace, yea, tidings of great joy, *how beautiful upon the mountains shall they be*" (1 Nephi 13:37; emphasis added).

Everyone who proclaims the gospel of Christ and who seeks to become a savior of men shall be a messenger with beautiful feet, whether standing upon the mountains or upon the plains. "What po-sition," asks Wilford Woodruff, "can any man occupy on the face of the earth, that is more noble, God-like, high and glorious than to be a messenger of salvation unto the human family?" (In *Journal of Dis-courses* 13:319.) The answer, of course, is an emphatic "None!"

It has been said that "the future of the race marches forward on the feet of little children" (Phillips Brooks, *Deseret News*). In one sense, this is a true statement. But in a broader sense, the future of all mankind marches forward on the feet of those "that bringeth good tidings of good; that publisheth salvation; that saith unto Zion, Thy God reigneth" (Mosiah 12:21). How very beautiful are the feet of those *who have, are still,* and *who shall hereafter* publish peace!

I close with my personal testimony of the divinity of missionary service, its sanctifying nature, and this stirring declaration: "Now, what do we hear in the gospel which we have received? A voice of gladness! A voice of mercy from heaven; and a voice of truth out of the earth; glad tidings for the dead; a voice of gladness for the living and the dead; glad tidings of great joy. How beautiful upon the moun-tains are the feet of those that bring glad tidings of good things, and that say unto Zion: Behold, thy God reigneth! As the dews of Carmel, so shall the knowledge of God descend upon them!" (D&C 128:19.)

INDEX